Maeve Higgins

OFF YOU GO

Away from home and loving it.

Sort of.

HACHETTE
BOOKS
IRELAND

First published in 2015 by Hachette Books Ireland
A division of Hachette UK Ltd

A CIP catalogue record for this title is available from the British Library.

ISBN 978 1 473 60981 5

Typeset by Bookends Publishing Services, Dublin
Cover design by headdesign.co.uk
Cover photo by Mindy Tucker www.withreservation.com

Printed and bound in Great Britain by CPI Group (UK) Ltd, Croydon,
CR0 4YY

Hachette Books Ireland policy is to use papers that are natural, renewable
and recyclable products and made from wood grown in sustainable forests.
The logging and manufacturing processes are expected to conform to the
environmental regulations of the country of origin.

Hachette Books Ireland
8 Castlecourt Centre, Castleknock
Dublin 15, Ireland

A division of Hachette UK Ltd
Carmelite House, 50 Victoria Embankment, London EC4Y 0DZ

www.hachette.ie

For Ettie

'And though she be but little, she is fierce.'

Contents

'Now, sweet one,
Be wise.
Cast all your votes for Dancing!'

Hafiz

What is Quark?

When I'm outside of Ireland and people hear my accent they think I'm either from *Game of Thrones* or from the past. I tell them they are wrong on both counts then I command them to guess again. Before they get a chance to do so I yell, 'I'm from Cork.'

'Like, uh, a cork in a wine bottle?' they ask. 'Exactly!' I say. 'If that wine bottle is Ireland and that cork has a capital C and is at the bottom of the wine bottle which is actually a country!'

An Australian girl at a party gasped with delight when I said I was from Cork. 'Like the cheese?' she asked. 'Is that where the cheese is from?' I felt a swell of pride, thinking she meant one of those crazy good cheeses made by Dutch lesbians who moved to the gentle fertile land of West Cork in the 1970s. That pride fell away as she continued. 'Quark, right?' I narrowed my eyes. Quark? Is that even cheese? It sounds like some type of punishment. 'Wrong,' I told her, my manner cool. Cool like the flagstones of an old stone dairy that would not dare to support the creation of anything other than a semi-soft cheese with a washed rind, a cheese with a light mushroom and nutty aftertaste, a cheese that deepens in flavour as it matures. I moved away from the Australian girl, leaving her with a classic parting shot. 'In Cork, we don't even know what quark is.'

And what *is* quark? No, sorry, I meant to say, and what *is* Cork? Oh, where to begin, this could take all night! Well, the county of Cork is your basic paradise. We've got it all – you can swim and surf and ski to your heart's desire – maybe not ski but you can certainly book a ski holiday from any one of the many travel agents that have somehow survived the digital age. The city is pocket-sized and perfect, with two restaurants per head of population and a market selling every good thing. Amongst the winding hills and ringing church bells of Shandon, you will find a museum dedicated to butter and a milk market that's become a theatre. Disneyland can burn to the ground, for there is no kingdom more magical than one built on dairy.

Cork is the BIGGEST and BEST county in Ireland. I'm the happiest girl in the world because I come from Cork. It's so nice and sunny and everyone is lovely. I love the food here. I wish everyone can live in Cork.
Miguel, 9 ½

That's just one extract from one fictional child's made-up diary, but I think it really sets the tone of just how I feel about Cork. You know how Frodo had the Shire, and he was always going on about it and wishing he were back there? That's just how Cork people feel when we are outside of Cork. We too have curly hair and are brave and humble. We are kept strong in battle by the memories of rolling green hills and the promise of being reunited once more with our sweet-natured companions.

People say things like 'I hate the Cork accent', or, less often, 'I love the Cork accent', and I know at once they are imposters dressed as humans because *there is no single Cork accent*. The accent changes every mile or so. It's a nightmare for those of us who tread the boards. At this point, after a lot of work with a dialect coach, I can do three accents:

1. Cobh accent
2. Midleton accent
3. Carrigtwohill accent

What the whole of Cork's oral tradition does share is an insistence on reminding everyone what gender they are. This will prove problematic in the future when the very idea of gender has been vanquished, but for now it's all 'Alright, Boy' and 'How are you, Girl?' There is such affection there. When I get to Grand Parade and I hear that kind of talk, I think of Louis Armstrong singing, 'I see friends shaking hands, saying, how do you do? They're really saying … I love you.'

You, like me on occasion, may sometimes enjoy asking the tough questions. Questions like, 'Why doesn't that cat have any eyes?' Or, 'Will anyone ever live up to the crazy expectations Maeve has been projecting onto them?' We'll get to them, but for now here's a tough question that I'm not scared of answering. *Is there anything bad about Cork?* No. Absolutely not, nothing at all. Of course, this is only natural, a part of me is like, 'I want more. I want more Cork.' Then another part of me says, 'No, Cork is the perfect size.' Have you ever seen Sylvester Stallone in real life? I haven't, but a guy I was talking to in a pizza place in the West Village had. As I waited for my, um, salad to heat up, this guy told me that he was surprised at how small Sylvester Stallone is. I think Cork is the same: unexpectedly small but still a very durable star.

I urge you to travel to Cork City and to marvel at the dark-eyed charming storytellers that populate the streets and taverns there. Many of these enchanting creatures are likely to be my sisters but you must not approach those ones. Particularly please do not approach them and tell them that I sent you, because they hate that. 'F**k sake, Maeve,' they will say, on WhatsApp.

And don't just take my word for it! When England owned Ireland the reigning monarch would gift parts of our country to their fancy English friends and they always saved Cork for their besties, like Sir Walter Raleigh. He bravely helped to slaughter hundreds of Catholic soldiers after they had surrendered in battle and as his reward he got to pretty much own East Cork! Using that logic, with some tweaks including 'no killing', I suppose I see Cork as the ultimate prize. For now I'll stay out here in the world and keep doing my thing. All being well I will get to go home again, home to Cork; with its beautiful soil and fabulous sunsets and fresh, fresh cream. And I'll be like, 'Finally! I earned this.'

A Christmas Miracle

A lot goes on in the giddy days and nights leading up to Christmas Day, particularly if you're young or single or pretending to be either or pretending to be both. There's so many parties, so much mistletoe, and that looming deadline of New Year's Eve makes everybody that bit more … approachable. Had you seen me clipping down Dublin's O'Connell Street around that time of year, you'd have said to yourself, possibly in a Prohibition-style gangster voice, 'Say, here comes a Yuletide honey now – that girl sure is ready for Kissmass.' Well, cool accent … but you're wrong. I was actually rushing along, squinting against the icy wind, trying to get to the cinema in time to see *Twilight: Breaking Dawn Part 2*.

That was my big hurry on 22 December, a vampire/wolf teen romance … on my own. I passed the nativity scene by the Spire, fenced in by chicken-wire on a traffic island, just like it was in old Bethlehem. Most of the major players were represented – Mary, Joseph, the donkey – but Jesus wasn't born yet, so they all gazed with fixed adoration into an empty crib. A baby due in a few days, but Mary still wasn't showing. A Christmas miracle! Across the street, lying face down on the dirty frozen footpath, was a large, red-haired man. Like everyone around me, I slowed down but kept walking. These were my thoughts upon seeing him, in the order that I thought them.

1. I've never done a first aid course.
2. I could try to help, but what if he wakes up and punches me?
3. I don't want to miss the part where the adult wolf falls in love with the vampire baby. I'm already late and I still have to buy Maltesers in the shop because cinema snacks are so over-priced!
4. What if that man is dead?
5. What if there are cameras and they play footage on the news of me running past the man's dead body to get to the cinema?

That last one stopped me cold. I could see the headlines already. 'Sad woman ignores dead man at Christmas to go see *Twilight: Breaking Dawn Part 2* – alone'. I ran back, knelt beside the man and said 'Excuse me, Mister', loudly. Nothing. I looked down at the man. His tracksuit was too small for him, his face and hands were dirty in that gotten-used-to-it way. He smelled like cider and the city. I took off my mittens and pressed his wrist, looking for a pulse. I couldn't feel one.

Then I pressed my own wrist and couldn't feel a pulse there either.

A man carrying a large Lidl shopping bag came and knelt beside me and said, in a French accent, 'The ambulance are coming, I call them.' I asked him if the man was dead.

'No,' he said. 'See how he is warm … and breathing so heavily.'

I did a little laugh, as if I'd made a joke that he didn't get, then I told the Frenchman that I had to go, I was meeting somebody.

Before I got a chance to leave, an old man, wild-eyed with a high-pitched voice, came hobbling over, saying, 'What's this – is he dead?'

He began poking at the unconscious man with his walking stick. I said, 'Hardly – he's warm and breathing quite heavily.'

The Frenchman added, 'Do not worry, Madame, the ambulance is coming, I called them.'

The thing was, the old man was androgynous-looking, not in a sulky he/she model kind of way. More like a light beard as well as large bosom kind of way. Fortunately the busty old man didn't notice the mix-up, he was too distracted by the other man's accent.

'Ah listen to you – we call you Froggies.'

The Frenchman missed the slur, but unfortunately inquired after it.

'Ah – I am sorry, Madame, you are speaking a little too fast.' Realising suddenly that he had been mistaken for a woman, the old man was irate.

'Madame? You're callin' me Madame? Are you blind, Froggie? I'm no Madame.'

Confusion fell over Le Bon Samaritain. 'Excuse me, Madame?'

'I am a *fella* and you are a blind froggie so you are.'

The Frenchman looked beseechingly at me for a translation.

So I said, as kindly as I could manage, 'This is a man, not a woman. He says you are a blind frog, a frog that cannot see.'

I covered my eyes and did a hopping motion to illustrate the point.

The Frenchman apologised and said he was indeed a blind frog. The old man softened.

'It's alright – everyone thinks I'm a girl. It's because of my hair.'

My eyes were drawn once more to his chest, but I hate

when guys do that to me, so I looked him in the eye and said, 'Yeah – that must be it.'

And so we stood there. The three wise men reluctantly taking care of our giant, hammered Baby Jesus asleep on the road. Eventually the medics arrived and shone a torch into the fallen man's eyes. As he stirred, one of them asked, 'Where were you going before you fell over?'

He came to, dazzled by the torch and the twinkling Christmas lights overhead and said, in just about the saddest voice I'd ever heard, 'Home – I was going home.'

My heart, finally and correctly, went out to him.

'Where's home?' Asked the medic. Everyone leaned in, waiting, and the man said, 'Ah, it's Egypt – where'd you think?'

We all exhaled and the medic replied, 'Oh fabulous, I hear Egypt is lovely this time of year.'

I walked away as the stacked old man claimed the Lidl shopping bag as his, and the Frenchman politely described its contents to a policeman to prove ownership. As I crossed the street to the cinema I believe I heard him mention fennel.

London Falling

I moved to Dublin in the year 2000. That sounds like it's in the future, but those of us in the know realise that it's actually in the past. I lived on Windmill Lane, in a little boxy flat in a big boxy building, right next to the Windmill Lane studios where luminaries like U2 and The Corrs used to record. The wall outside my flat was covered in graffiti, mainly complimenting U2. It had become a tourist tradition to scrawl things there, and it was handy for residents too. In amongst the 'Larry Mullen remember Siena '88? Me pregnant', you can still see where I jotted down little reminders to myself, like 'buy credit' or 'get tanning gloves'. That last one is near a large, orange handprint, like one a bronzed orc would make having rested there for a moment before continuing his hunt for halflings.

The skinny balcony clinging to my third floor flat looked out across the Liffey quays and all I could see were cranes.

There were so many cranes, their long necks crossed each other on the skyline, swinging skips and girders around like they were made of styrofoam. Giant cranes and regular-sized ones, there was even a miniature crane squatting on a barge in the river – all of them were busy, all day, every day. After a few years I got so used to them that I didn't even notice that they'd left. They must have loped off silently. After that, things in Dublin got really quiet.

I moved to London in 2013, partially because of this quietness. Walking up Kings Cross Road a couple of weeks after I had moved there, I spotted the cranes. I looked up, and saw their scrawny necks crossing a different skyline – busy again – with their bales of blocks and huge steel rods. They'd scarpered off to England! I called them on it.

'Hey you – this is where you've been hiding?' They swivelled around. 'No hard feelings mate, we done what we could but there was nothing there for us no more.' I was indignant – the cheek of them. The going got tough, and they got out. I watched them build their new lives and I felt angry. Usually when I resent something or someone, it's because some part of me identifies only too well with them, and the cranes were no exception.

I too had abandoned Dublin. My darling Dublin, we had all fled! Who was left to make stupid jokes in the upstairs room of a pub? Lots of people, too many in fact, but you must allow me my keening rights. Every Irish emigrant is obliged to feel at least a little bit sad and just a touch ashamed about being away from home.

When I was a small girl, my father left to work as a surveyor on a construction site in London. Myself and my sisters and brother hated this city that took him away. That said, we loved the treats he brought back, McCoys crisps and Rose's lime marmalade. He assured us that he didn't talk to anyone while he was there – instead he just did his work, had his dinner, phoned us and went to bed. Sometimes he visited his sister. We were happy enough with that. Like so many others, my father went to a city to get something from it, to better his family's situation and, crucially, to come home again.

Lots of Irish men worked on the building sites of London in the 1940s and 1950s, and many never made it back. I watched a documentary about their plight and learned that many of those men were so lonely and isolated in the city that they turned to drink, then they lost their jobs and their teeth fell out. They were too broke and too mortified to come home to Ireland and instead vanished into the city. I asked my sister if she thought this might happen to me. She did that thing of saying my name then repeating back to me what I had just said in a flat tone of voice: 'Maeve. You're asking if I think you will be so lonely in your job as a bricklayer that you'll turn into an alcoholic and be too embarrassed to come home because you don't have any teeth?

I hate when she does that.

I never *wanted* to move to London. I decided to move there because it was time to leave Dublin and London seemed easy and obvious – it is close, I have friends there, it would be good for my career. Those were fine reasons but they didn't fill me with enthusiasm, which, it turns out, is a vital ingredient for a good start in a new place. In Dublin, London can feel like an older brother who used to bully you, someone who tormented you just enough that you will never fully like or trust him, but not so much that you don't still think he's cool, and secretly hope that one day he'll think that you're cool too.

I do not take that big brother of mine for granted. I know he'll be there when I need him. Irish and English people speak the same language and are allowed to work freely in one another's countries. I was glad of that the morning I showed up at the Camden Town Job Centre with my paperwork and a carefully rehearsed version of 'my circumstances'. Hordes of people stood outside, looking confused and speaking a dozen different languages. The fire alarm was going off. What a thrill, to live in a country where people take fire alarms seriously! I joined what I thought was a queue but turned out to be a Spanish family having a picnic. Just as they finished the tortilla, the alarm stopped and everyone filed in. I showed my passport and appointment letter to a security man and he sent me upstairs. After a long wait, mainly spent avoiding eye contact with an intense Armenian baby glaring at me from a pram, my name was called.

A smiley, softly spoken woman asked me what I planned on doing while I was in the United Kingdom. I told her I hoped to get work writing comedy. She asked me if I liked the television show *Blackadder* and I said I did, though in truth, I don't really know it at all. Then she said, 'One day we may see your name in the credits of *Blackadder*!' I didn't mention the one thing I did know about *Blackadder* – that they stopped writing it in the 1980s. Instead I said brightly, 'I hope so!' and skipped out of the building. My National Insurance Number arrived in the post shortly afterwards. I wasn't sure how to celebrate it. Perhaps I should get a cake? A tattoo? Oh, or maybe a job?

I never settled into a job, not really. I did a few shows, but I wasn't feeling any compulsion to perform. Perhaps the effort of establishing myself in a city as huge and disinterested as London was too much but, creatively speaking, the sheer volume of posh English boys doing bad stand-up comedy chilled me to the core, and the panel-show frenzy happening on television could not have been less appealing. I didn't want to make anyone laugh, not like that.

I did write, I did, but it was difficult and slow. Whole days went by when I sat in my tiny, expensive room in Hackney, with actual woodchip on the wall, gazing at a blinking, empty screen and wondering if I'd made the right choice. I imagined other realities. In the multiverse of my life I could easily have stayed in Cobh and had a scatter of distracting and adorable babies instead, like my sisters and my friends had. I spent a lot of time caught between alternating pillars of fantasy and regret. I can't blame London for that. My maudlin Irish character surely played a part in that, but let's not bring Gertie into this. She gets so down on herself as it is.

The question is: why didn't things work out between London and me? Let's examine the evidence and rate each piece on points. May the best entity win!

LONDON VS MAEVE

The case FOR London

1. Possibility of adventure

The most fun I had during the entire year I lived in London was when I left London and went to Kent, of all places. I am, however, including this in the FOR column because the adventure began and ended in the city.

My newly single friend, with all the recklessness of the recently heartbroken, had planned this micro-adventure to distract herself from the rotten feeling of love gone awry and I had promised to go with her. Micro-adventures begin after work – so to be authentic we agreed to pretend we were office workers and not leave until the office was closed. It is then that you must get out of the city, by bike or foot or public transport, walk to a scenic spot, make a camp (no tents allowed, just you and a sleeping bag), have your dinner, maybe light a campfire, and go to sleep.

The next morning you wake up, swim in a river and go back to work with leaves in your hair and smelling slightly like smoke, hopefully smiling to yourself in a way that maddens others.

My brilliant, sad friend and I set off from Liverpool Street station at 5pm and an hour and a half later, much to my sunlit amazement, we were tramping through golden fields being chirruped at by birds. We messed and skipped and puffed our way along a pretty little river and scared each other with potential adventure enders, featuring murderers, slugs and distracted combine-harvester drivers. At around 9.30pm we chose a place to sleep: the top corner of a stubbly cornfield, near a group of sturdy elms which waved and bowed in welcome. We ate our picnic, a strange collection of hummus, fruit and ham, and bedded down for the night.

I hadn't brought a bivvy bag. In truth I had thought that bivvy bag was another word for sleeping bag. I didn't realise it was a bigger, heavier plastic bag that stops the damp and cold from seeping into your actual sleeping bag. My friend, a seasoned camper, wrapped my sleeping bag in black bin liners instead. She seemed dubious about my chance of survival, but we had a good old laugh about it. Then we lay under a big sky of dusky light, filled with little flitting bats and little stars that popped out one by one, reporting for cosmic duty. Some were late for work, and shot across the sky busily as we yelled beneath them. I fell asleep easily. A few hours later, the cold woke me. I was absolutely freezing, so cold it was hard to move my limbs around. I put on a polo neck and a hat, pulled the bin liners a little closer (stop me if you're getting too turned on) and felt much better, like maybe I'd make it through the night. And I did!

We woke early the next morning, to sounds of a tractor in the field above us. After packing up, we went swimming in the river. It was my first time actually being in a river, not beside it or on it or looking at it. I was actually in it. Getting in was difficult, slipping between reeds and trying to find my footing on the silty riverbed. The water was cool and murky, with little flies buzzing as they hovered just above the surface. I swam for a while then I stayed very still, like a crocodile.

We got dressed and walked back through the fields to the station. We ate nectarines on the train, looking like any other commuter with muddy feet and matted hair.

For this experience I award London 200 shooting stars.

2. Low-cost pills and free chats

I went to the doctor in London. I cannot tell you why. Although, what you're imagining is probably far more embarrassing than the reason. No, I didn't suffer an anxiety induced fart attack. That hasn't happened since I was 30. It's not gossip-worthy either. Despite rumours, I am not pregnant with Michael Fassbender's triplets. This top is just a little bit baggy and he and I are keeping things casual – for now. OK, OK! I will say we are discussing having kids. He wants them, but I'm undecided because my acting career is going so well. Please, our publicist would kill me if she heard me telling you that, so don't let the tabloids get a hold of this, I beg you. I went to the doctor for no reason other than that it is totally free to shoot the breeze with a medical professional and who doesn't love a good, one-sided conversation about themselves?

I registered with my local GP in Hackney and the nurse took down my address and gave me a little plastic vial. I knew what it was for immediately – a transparent home for my new pet bee! 'Afraid not,' she whispered, 'diabetes is on the rise.' I couldn't hear her, so she shouted it. 'DIABETES IS ON THE RISE.' It's ringing in my ears still. Worth it, though, because I got free healthcare!

One of the more frustrating parts of being me is my limited understanding of how the world works. Certain things make absolute sense to me and I think very little about them. I understand why jokes work and how to behave on an airplane and the reason we pay taxes. I know that butter makes everything delicious and looking at water calms me down. Other things make me squint and sigh as I try to figure them out. The three most persistent knots I cannot unpick are people who drink cans of beer on trains, grape-flavoured sweets and health insurance. For years, my father urged me to sort out my health insurance, to get my own plan. I told him to relax and explained that I had a plan. My plan was to see what happened and worry about it then. Not ideal. So now, I say it loud: 'God Save the NHS.'

I give London eleven urine samples for its humane healthcare system.

3. One night of generosity

I was doing a show at a comedy festival in Peterborough, because that's what happens when you make it in show business.

After the show, one of the comedians gave me a spin home in his Jaguar (the car, not the creature). Not home exactly, he dropped me as far as West London and I lived on the other side, over an hour away. Still, there was an apple rolling around the back seat and he said I could have it. Then I got a night bus to Piccadilly Circus where I remembered I hadn't printed off my boarding card for my flight to Dublin the next morning. It was 1am and I wandered into a Holiday

Inn. The night manager was alone in the lobby, anxiously watching some kids that were drinking cans outside. I said I needed to use the printer and he asked if I was staying at the hotel. I didn't lie exactly, but I did nod. He waved me toward the printer distractedly. Boarding card in hand, I went to get another bus home, but realised I didn't have change. I asked a man for change of a tenner at the bus stop; he didn't have any so he just gave me the fare. So, I got a guided tour of Peterborough, four pages printed, a spin in a Jaguar, £2 and an apple – all for free, all in one day. I was giddy after this crazy parade of kindness in England – the friendliest place on Earth.

I award London three tins of Bulmers for this unprecedented show of good heartedness.

The case AGAINST London

1. Lack of human contact

Every single week a Tube carriage full of people moves to London. I can't say I have it tough in any real way – like those early Irish emigrants did, or someone working as a kitchen porter for a fiver an hour with a recurring kidney infection and not a word of English, or a refugee, or a Welsh person – can you imagine being Welsh? Even when you're a total legend like myself, it's hard work convincing strangers that you're worth knowing. At the beginning, I felt like I was butting into people – that dreaded little billygoat looking for conversation.

'Hi,' I say to them, blocking their path at a party where I only know the host and he's busy. 'How are you? I'm Maeve, just moved to London.' It's a terrible opener, and the tinny need in my voice makes us both flinch. This is what happens when you move to a new place – you have to make new friends. You go to things you don't want to go to, and force yourself to take off your coat and make small talk. You are friendly and warm, so agreeable!

I did all of those things. I did them so much that the thought crossed my mind that I might be a sociopath; all empty charm using flattery to get what I wanted. I fretted about that until I realised it wasn't working – I wasn't gathering a new tribe around me. So if I was a sociopath, I was bad at it. I took some comfort in that fact.

Charlotte Bronte had Jane Eyre say, '*I care for myself. The more solitary, the more friendless, the more unsustained I am, the more I will respect myself.*' I love that. Also, of course, she got the lead in a film *and* fooled around with Michael Fassbender. That being said, Jane could have done with some pals to guide her, make her laugh, explain what a diva cup is and generally keep her company.

Here is what friendship is to me. I am my heart, my family is my blood and my work is my brain – friendship is the part that animates me – people are my energy. The steady connection to people I didn't always know, people I have chosen and who have chosen me back, people I want to impress and understand and be with as they make their way around this world, thrilled they're here the same time as me. Old friends tread beside me on a path of forgiveness and warmth and shared experience while new friends open laneways I didn't know were there, and force me to figure out what I'm about as I polish up the best parts of me and hope they accept the worst.

Don't get me wrong – there were loads of great people in my new English life. There was my downstairs neighbour, a completely silent woman, always hanging out her washing. My GP seemed nice, though he was always away on holiday. And there were the mice, as well as any number of rats and foxes, peeping in at me from the garden.

Making is a verb, of course, an action. In London, I didn't take any action – I didn't make any friends. That's on me, and probably has something to do with how close I was to home. The proximity to Ireland allowed me not to put down roots. That said, it's also got something to do with the city itself – London did not show me the same curiosity and welcome that New York has. Here, I've made so many friends I feel like I've won the lottery, but instead of millions of dollars there are hundreds of moments – moments of understanding, laughing, gossiping, working and learning.

There's a certain streak of superiority felt in Europe,

one that says with tight-lipped derision, 'Ugh, that's so *American*,' about qualities like openness and positivity. It's so easy to be lazily cynical about the phrase, 'Have a nice day,' and those who utter it, but the fact remains that I've had countless nice days on this side of the Atlantic and don't plan on stopping any time soon.

2. Not so happy birthday

In merry old London, I'll tell you how I spent my birthday. I went for lunch in Ottolenghi and ate a salad that cost more than my jeans. Granted, the jeans in question were on sale in Primark and had a rip in the inside leg. Then I went to the cinema. I spent the whole day on my own. Look, that is all fine. I like being alone. The only time I felt weird about it was when I spoke to my parents that night. Here's how the Skype call went.

MAEVE
(*cartoon voice*)
Hi Memmy, hi Deddy.

MOTHER
Hi sweetheart.
Happy birthday – we were waiting for you to ring!

MAEVE
(*irritated voice*)
Oh! Well you could always ring me.

MOTHER
(*tiny voice*)
Sure we don't know how this thing works, lovey.

MAEVE
(*let's pick this up voice*)
Right. Well, how are ye?

MOTHER
We're fine, love, Daddy's tired.

MAEVE
Oh yeah – was he working?

MOTHER
He was. Yes. And he dug up the back garden and put down a new layer of mulch.

MAEVE
And can he not tell me that himself?

EVERYONE
Laughing for ages.

MOTHER
What did you do today?

MAEVE
(*high, lying voice*)
I'd a gorgeous lunch and then went to the cinema so it was fabulous I must say!

MOTHER/MAEVE
In-depth discussion of food – 10 mins long.

MOTHER
And who else was there?

MAEVE
(barely staying calm voice)
Ummm. A big gang of us? Loads of people showed up in the end – the waiters were going crazy because they had to keep bringing chairs to our table. My whole crew!

MOTHER
(Hollywood villain voice)
Like who, pet?

MAEVE
(panicked criminal voice)
Ah … you wouldn't know them like – they're just friends like Murakami she's a Japanese girl and then some of the lads upstairs they're gas and then just like Lydia and Mike. Oh I better go here because my phone battery is running low.

MOTHER
(knowing when to drop it voice)
Oh silly me, thought you were on your computer.
All right – love you and happy birthday!

MICHAEL FASSBENDER OFF-CAMERA
(*gruff 'just had sex' voice*)
Maeve – would you get back in here and do the work I'm paying you for?

MAEVE
(*stricken but pleased voice*)
Bye – love you too!

FATHER
Turns his head to the side quizzically, opens his mouth to say something. Fade to black.

I deduct London town upwards of 15 relighting candles for this sorry affair.

3. Public transport

I sometimes got bullied on the Number 40 bus that took me from Kilmainham to Dublin city centre. One day, two squirrelly looking girl-women that may have been mother and daughter or may have been sisters yelled at me for the duration of the 15-minute trip into town. Forgive my rendering of their patois, but it will help you to hear what I heard. 'Dere's your one off da telly tinkin she's real famous and all, and da state of her fuckin phone, an aul Nokia.' So I cannot in truth say I miss Dublin's public transport.

In 2011, mysterious screens began appearing at bus stops

around Dublin city centre. Nobody knew what the screens were for; neighbourhood gossip speculated wildly. Were they weather warnings, the names of people who didn't recycle or, perhaps, were they tiny, communal TVs? A great hush descended as we watched them flicker to life and … announce how long the wait for the next bus would be. Genius! At my local stop on Kingsland Road in London there were multiple screens with lists of buses that stopped almost every minute. This sorcery was taken for granted. People actually tutted and scuffed if they had to wait more than three minutes for a bus. Their impatience bothered me more than the haranguing I got on the number 40. They couldn't wait three minutes – that's how important Londoners are! That's how annoying they are.

The public transport system is wonderful, but it's full of the public. For that I award London three rotten oysters.

Concluding Remarks and Verdict

The reasons I've moved to every city I've lived in are universal – ambition, boredom, a change and a certain type of freedom. There is also this feeling that's hard to explain but is perhaps the defining one of my life. It's similar to the feeling I get when there's a photo being passed around a table and I'm waiting my turn to see it. I'm anticipating seeing it, I'm watching other people experience it and imagining what they are feeling and I can't wait and then

I finally get my hands on it and … I don't get it. *That's it?*
I think. *Am I'm missing something? Is there another one, a*
better one?

That's a lot of pressure to put on one little city in England.
In conclusion, both parties lose; London is found guilty of
not embracing Maeve, but she has to pay costs.

Gardening in London
When You're Lonely

House-hunting in London is a curiously unhealthy combination of adrenaline and tedium. I spent two months traipsing around to places that turned out not to exist and places that did exist but only in an alternative universe where I was a princess from Doha with oil money to burn. I was baffled by the rental market but had to find somewhere to put my things. Well, somewhere to put myself more than my things. Before I left Dublin I gave away almost everything – my furniture, my plants, my secrets. I held on to what I needed, which apparently was one entire suitcase of gym gear that had mysteriously gotten too tight to wear (peanut butter straight from the jar perhaps?) and four champagne glasses. Not champagne flutes; I can't bear those nose-catching flimsy-stemmed flamingo-looking numbers. These four glasses were round and flat, and made it easy to pretend to be Bette Davis circa 1949 toasting another great role for women over the age of 40, as long as it wasn't for Joan Crawford.

On and on went the bonkers rounds of viewings and unfathomable exchanges with demented estate agents. My sublet ended and I stayed in a friend's place in Dalston while she was away. I tried on one of her dresses and somehow, ripped the seams (eating peanut butter from a jar again perhaps – who can truly know?). As I sat sewing up the busted dress, I looked at her little deck out the back, covered in hanging branches with a dejected-looking barbecue standing in the middle, unsure of what would happen next. I didn't have the heart to tell it that I knew just what would happen next so I whispered it. *Nothing will happen next little grill – nobody will ever use you again because they are too busy working to get enough money to pay for the yard you stand in.*

When I say the estate agents were demented I don't mean it in a bad way. It's easy to rag on that profession, but what I came to understand is that it's not really their fault. Estate agents in London have to think about money and moving and more money and more moving, all day every day. It's a crazy whirl that spins up and up with no resting place between floors. I'd be demented too. At the beginning of my third month of searching, I went back to Ireland for the weekend. I was staying in my family home peeling the inevitable potatoes when I got a text from my flatmate in London saying she had found us a place, followed by three wads of cash with wings and a sunflower in emojis. I understood from her missive that the place was crazy expensive and it had a garden. After all this time it came down to my texted response. Starchy water pooled on my phone as I sent her back a simple smiley face with a tiny gun pointing to it. I hoped this would convey my excitement.

The apartment was *almost* in Stoke Newington and had *almost* exactly doubled in rent since the last lease, three years previously. I knew this because Matt, the handsome, dopey estate agent, sent us the previous tenant's lease by accident. His boss, a woman named Tugboat, didn't let him deal with us after that. After the frenzy of paperwork and security checks and the wrangling over which furniture was the least ugly – he disappeared. Almost disappeared; I did see him one more time when he called over to check on the mouse issue.

You see, as soon as we moved into the house, we saw a mouse. Then we saw him again. Or perhaps there was more than one mouse. A mouse striking out alone, away from the watchful gaze of his controlling mouse parents, all grown up and living independently – in an almost good part of town? Not likely. It just seemed like there was just one because whenever we saw a mouse it seemed to be the same one. Look, I'm going to say this, to hell with political correctness

"Women are
smarte

– they all look the same. They don't go to the trouble of getting their ears pierced so we can tell them apart, so why should I tiptoe around their feelings?

It turned out there was an actual colony of little English mice living under the kitchen sink. That's how it happened that Matt came to investigate whether or not we were making this up, and found me on the front steps in the sun. We sat there together for a while in a pretty nice silence. He asked me what I did for a living and I said I was a writer, and he said, 'Oh yeah? Is that why your mate had to sign security for you – cos you're out here in the sun instead of up on your typewriter doing your work?' I said that was exactly why. We then went back to a less nice silence, until he asked why I wasn't using the back garden. I showed him the garden through our kitchen window – the brand new sun had made it go crazy. It was tangled and overgrown and all the trellising had blown down. 'Anyway,' I explained 'A mother fox lives in the thorns at the end with two baby foxes so I don't want to scare them.' Matt shook his head and said to expect a call from Tugboat to set up an appointment with The Exterminator. He laughed at my horrified expression and said, 'For the mice, darling, not the foxes.'

Tugboat called and asked if there was anyone available to let The Exterminator into the house the following week. I explained to her that I was always at home. 'Good,' she said in her brisk way that made it sound like everything was going to be fine, 'I'll send him round.' I didn't fully trust her because despite her professional tone she often bent the truth, like when we asked for new curtains and she agreed to send them, but then ancient, tiny curtains arrived, smelling of smoke and slightly too short for the windows. The curtains made the house look like an old man who had rolled up his trousers to go for a paddle.

On the mouse front, Tugboat sailed through. The Exterminator arrived with a convincing-looking rucksack filled with various plastic tubs of different coloured powder that he distributed behind the fridge and under the floorboards. We made small talk, he said he was Turkish and I told him I was Irish – he said he heard Obama had visited Ireland recently.

'He is a brave man. Maybe one of your crazy peoples would kill him, no? But he go visit anyway.'

I felt a mighty need to defend my nation's reputation, so I said, 'Oh I don't know, I don't think any of my crazy peoples would do that.'

The Exterminator shrugged and kept doling out the poison. 'I am not really a pest control guy, I am in college you know? Studying law, finance, things like that.'

I was pleased to hear he wasn't a dedicated killer, because I wanted the mice to live. I liked their company. In the end, just one mouse died, clutching his little chest as he crawled out from under the oven. His family didn't mourn him for long – the partying continued beneath the floorboards. Tugboat promised to send The Exterminator back to get the rest, but he never appeared. I imagine him in a stylish start-up office inside a converted warehouse somewhere along Canary Wharf, his backpack slung over a bean bag as he gets busy with 'law, finance, things like that'.

We lived in the house through the burning hot summer and never used the garden. My flatmates went to work and I would gaze at it from the window, to see how the fox cubs were doing. They wrestled with each other and pounced through the brambles. They grew big and strong. I resisted naming them and counting them as friends. I felt a dull guilt about the garden. I kept meaning to *do something about it*. That vague and exasperating feeling was not limited to the garden – that poor old patch of neglected ground was a symbol of a reality stretching to pretty much every part of me at that time. That hum of *I must do something about it* haunted me through the hottest and loneliest summer of my life.

That is, of my life so far!

I had to leave London. The friends I lived with were kind about it – I suppose they could see I was wilting. But I was determined to get the garden cleared before I went and this decision took on an exaggerated importance in my mind. I found an ad on Gumtree that read:

'Sorya – all garden and build – £20 an hour.'

I trust people who go under one name because it means their brand is strong. Sorya was indeed a hero. He showed up the next morning as I packed my bags – a gigantic man with baleful eyes, puffing up the steps like some kind of saviour in a white tracksuit. He was holding a strimmer in one hand, bouncing a wheelbarrow behind him with the other. As he smoked a cigarette to get his breath back, I asked him to clear everything except the fox den. Two hours later, the place was flattened. I went outside with a mug of tea and a glass of water for Sorya and stood in awe on the brand new carpet of torn-up shrubs and weeds and nettles. Flies buzzed around frantically and the air smelled of recent violence. Sorya refused the water but downed his tea before he began shovelling the detritus into his wheelbarrow.

As I turned to go inside, I saw a huge, beautiful bunch of grapes glistening, perfectly intact amongst the wreckage. I had no idea how they'd gotten there, these dark rubies straight from a painting. I leaned to pick them up and asked Sorya if they were his, if he'd brought them. He squinted at them and said no. He explained that there were three vines full of grapes and he'd pulled them down as instructed.

Gardening lends itself to metaphor embarrassingly easily. Cultivating, growing, nurturing – I will spare you. Suffice to say that part of me regrets not thinking to look for treasure in the ruins and part of me is comforted by finding out it was there all along. I don't know. I do know that I stood there for a long time, uncomfortably shifting in my too-tight running leggings, drinking chlorinated London water from a champagne glass, watching a man tip the contents of his wheelbarrow, jewels and all, into the bin.

Silent Night

'Which of the boys slept in this bed do you suppose?' I desperately wanted to quote that line, dreamily uttered by Dorcas Galen in *Seven Brides for Seven Brothers*, but I couldn't, because I'd taken a vow of silence for ten days. I lay mute in the bottom bunk-bed, grossing myself out with potential answers to that question. Since it was in a boys' boarding school, I knew this narrow little mattress was probably the victim of many teenage boys down through the years, masturbating furiously until the break of dawn. Grimacing with the cold and a general sense of 'ewwww', I zipped my sleeping bag right over my shoulders and pulled up my hood. It was the day after Christmas and I had made a mistake. I should never have come here. My roommate swung her legs over the side of her bed and wordlessly turned off the light. A moonbeam shone through a crack in the blind and perfectly illuminated a line of graffiti scrawled onto the wooden slats of the bunk above: 'You have a tiny dick.'

I got colder and further from sleep as I relived my day. I was back from London for Christmas and had woken up in my childhood bedroom. That morning I had eaten a crazy breakfast with my giant family, a classic Christmas leftovers meal that included bread sauce and roasted sprouts with lardons and possibly, no, definitely, plum pudding with brandy butter. Then I had reluctantly packed a bag using the list provided by the retreat directors as a very rough guideline. They said to bring things like an alarm clock, a Thermos, a shawl and other 1970s relics I don't own, so I just made sure to bring my phone charger.

My sister Raedi dropped me at the bus station. Raedi is one of those people I can't trick, unfortunately. 'Tell me again what you are doing,' she said, her face clouding with concern when I explained my plan.

'Look, it's totally fine even though actually I just remembered we're not allowed to use our phones but if anything happens at home just phone the boys' school in Ennis.' I couldn't recall the name of the school where the retreat was taking place and this worried her further, so I put my hand on her leg and said, 'Girl, if I don't like it I can just climb out the window or something.' She moved my hand because she hates when I do that. 'You'll miss your bus, Maeve, if you don't hurry.' I kissed her and jumped out of the car, leaving my scarf on the front seat. Raedi waved it at me but I didn't bother to get it. I cursed myself for that now – such a cosy scarf, such a cold night.

Ennis is a town in the west of Ireland known for fiddle music and fighting, and I wondered which was the bigger attraction for the hordes of people boarding the bus that morning. As for me – let's just say I can't stand the violin … I jammed my suitcase into the bowels of the bus and waited until last to get on, like I do with flights. The driver put his foot out on the step I was about to climb. 'Full up – sorry now but ye will have to make your own arrangements.'

I looked around for the other person in the 'ye', but didn't see anyone. 'Often by Limerick there's enough people gone that you could hop on then so maybe try getting there,' he suggested, pressing the door button to close the luggage compartments. I felt a giddy flood of relief. I had no way to get to Limerick, I was off the hook – no retreat! More brandy butter!

I hauled my bag out just before the doors shut, and in the process elbowed a tiny old man who had been shadowing me the entire time, too close and too small to be seen. 'I'm so sorry – I didn't see you!' I told him. The man had a baggy old anorak on, but underneath it I saw the combination that never fails to break my heart – a round-neck jumper over a shirt and tie, a bachelor farmer's best 'going out' clothes. He shook his little head and said, 'Not to worry, girlie – but isn't this some pickle, ha? How will we get to Limerick at all?'

I felt that curious blend of irritation and responsibility that happens when a stranger hops aboard your life for a while. 'Don't worry – we can go in and ask the man.' I said this assuredly, although I'm never quite sure who 'the man' is. The bus station was packed with people. I led the way, looking back to see that the little farmer was following. He winked and clicked his tongue at me as if he was instructing a sheepdog around a herd on some windy headland. I found a uniformed bus man who seemed deeply unhappy and offered us no clues as to how to get to Limerick in time to catch the Ennis bus.

I was about to call Raedi to ask her to come back and get me, and explain that I had taken into my care a tiny rural gentleman, when a smiling woman waved across the crowd. 'Paddy!' she called, and I instantly knew two things. One was that she was looking for my new companion; he could only be called Paddy. And two, I knew that this was his niece. I was correct: she had come back to check that he had made it onto the bus. We huddled against the crowd and explained to her what had happened. Without missing a beat she said she would drive us both to Limerick. 'What else would I be doing today?' she asked incredulously. 'Aren't I on my holidays?' Her backseat was full of baking trays and board games and running gear. Clues as to some of the other things she could be and was hoping to be doing that day. Surely more fun than driving Paddy and myself along the wet grey roads for an hour and a half. St Stephen's Day is one of the loveliest days of the year to spend at home; with the duties of Christmas all over you can just be still in the glow of it all.

So why the hell couldn't this blasted woman have been still in the glow of it? Oh no, instead here she was dragging me up to bloody Limerick where I *did* manage to get the bus to Ennis, where I *did* register with a lot of nervous-looking people for this Vipassanna retreat with its ten days of complete silence! I had undertaken this demented experiment because actual yoga retreats were too expensive, what a terrible reason! The bus was full because I should not be here. Yet the woman ruined it all. Why did she come back to check on Paddy, why infantilise the poor man like that? I wondered where he was that night, after we'd said our goodbyes in Limerick. I'm sure he was in a cute little cottage drinking warm milk and honey. Why wasn't I? Why had I agreed to come here to this freezing silent place where men and women were segregated? And now I had to wake up at 5am and I didn't even know how to do that because I didn't bring a stupid alarm clock because I don't even know where I would buy one because it's not the goddamned past.

The first day came and went in a confusing blur. A gong rang every few hours, we ate together in silence except for those of us who love to chew loudly and make scraping noises with our cutlery. Mainly, we meditated – or tried to. I had never meditated before and was not at all sure of what to do. Turns out it is super easy. You just close your eyes and think of all the people that betrayed you and hurt you then decide upon their punishment. Next, you think of all the people that annoy you but you can't explain why, and come up with an explanation strong enough to convince others to agree with you. Gradually move through to the people that never gave you the €12 they owed you for wine that time you all went drinking in your cousin's house when you were 19. You will reach complete Enlightenment as you revisit the time in Junior Infants when Mrs O'Connell held up a paper plate and asked what it looked like and Mikey Kelly said, 'The moon,' just as you said, 'The sun,' and she said 'That's right, Mikey – the moon.' You will remember with deep clarity that the indentations around the plate were exactly like the rays of the sun and the smooth paper centre was nothing like the cratered moon surface. Your moment of Zen will come when you know that you were right and Mikey was wrong and kindly old Mrs O'Connell had simply thrown him a bone because he was dyslexic and adopted.

That first night was a nightmare I could not sleep through or wake up from. The hours crawled by as every kind of unexpected and unwanted thought and memory and imagining came crashing into my brain. Some were tiny and repetitive, woodpeckers reminding me of the scarf left behind or a friendship gone sour. Others were larger and slower, vultures advancing surely on the tenderest parts of me, the ones best left alone, conjuring every inevitable loss. They pecked and tore at me busily through that night and the next, and the next, until I was sure those terrible birds would eat me right up. Only the sound of my roommate's breathing, even and human above me, kept me moored to the world and prevented those creatures from gripping the sheets with their beaks and winging my carcass up and through the night sky to their shadowy nests.

Well, that and the thought of breakfast the next morning. I mean, talk about delicious – the breakfast was totally magic! The relief at the dawn's appearance and the physical hunger from not having eaten dinner, because instead of dinner there is a banana, surely played their parts, but the food that appeared on the large table in the dining hall each morning was definitely enchanted. Ordinary to look at – vats of porridge, prunes in orange juice, toast with peanut butter – but tasting so exquisite I could swear that it was laid out by some tribe of secular angels wishing us well, willing us on.

The second and third days were spent getting used to the routine of a Vipassana retreat. They happen the same way all around the world. A gong is sounded to make sure everyone is awake, then it's meditation, then gong, then breakfast, then gong, then meditation, then gong, then meditation, then gong, then gong meditation gong meditation gong gong gong all day long, bossing us around. I liked that. No decisions, no explaining, no smiling, no eye contact, nobody else there really. Just me in my body surrounded by other people in theirs being cared for by the volunteers with their quiet careful hands and gentle blank faces.

In the nights I wondered if I was going crazy. That line from an Emily Dickinson poem about a plank breaking in reason boomed around my head over and over, at times even louder than the jabbering birds. I remembered reading somewhere that if you wonder whether or not you're going crazy, that means you're definitely not. Or maybe I read that when you wonder whether or not you're a psychopath then *that* means you're not a psychopath, because psychopaths don't mind if they are psychopaths. Their whole thing is, 'Yeah, so? I do whatever I want.' I had never wondered whether or not I was a psychopath, so there was a new worry, and did all of this mean perhaps I was going crazy after all? The histrionics came and went, just as the days and nights did, just as everything does.

Before I left for the retreat, my sister's boyfriend told me how 'one of the lads' – he has a collection of lads with extraordinary names like Kettle and Chief and Hopper – had done a 10-day Vipassana retreat in India and thought it was 'better than any trip he's done and he's done *everything*'.

My mother said she would love to do a retreat but didn't have the time because too many people need her. A guy in a pub on Christmas Eve said I shouldn't bother going, that his friend actually meditates by walking to the shop quite slowly, and that's all you need. I don't know what anyone needs, but I must echo Padjo or Rodey or Numbnuts or whatever that lad was called and say that this trip was better than any I'd done.

The year changed to a new one as I slept deeply on the sixth night. After that the time got blurry again. The retreat was like being at the bottom of a deep, still well but not in a frightening way, a well where you are able to move and breathe. On the last day the meditation teacher explained that it was time to break the Noble Silence. We could all meet in the dining hall and have tea and biscuits and look at each other and talk. The partition between men and women was removed. Talking was tricky. I couldn't quite remember my lines. Men were tricky too – same problem. My roommate, a brilliant Limerick girl, introduced herself and we laughed a lot, about everything. We talked like old friends, about breakups and sheepdogs and particularly about those never-ending nights at the beginning of the retreat. She thought I was asleep the whole time. I told her I couldn't sleep on account of the flock of birds tearing strips out of me. She said they got to her too, and we laughed some more.

Everybody helped to clean the school the next day, and I got a lift back to Cork in a tiny car that was stuffed with people and bags and pillows. The thunderous storms we heard during the retreat had done their worst and much of the farmland around Ennis was flooded. There were trees down and fences broken but it was over now, all that remained was a soft calm mist as we made our way home. And it was all still there. In Cork I sat in the train station marvelling at the tiling as the Cobh train came and went without me. I got the next one. The colours in my parents' kitchen were brighter and warmer than any I'd ever seen.

Absolutely Tiny
Aubergines

The rain had almost washed my name off of the blackboard outside The International Bar on Dublin's Wicklow Street but I could still make it out as I walked by. A woman behind me saw my name too, I heard her say, 'Oh look, Maeve is in town.' Nobody knew me in my new city, London, and I warmed to this voice that recognised my name, even if it was misspelled under a laminated photo of a toasted cheese sandwich. I was back in Dublin for a weekend of shows at the comedy club upstairs in The International – a small room painted black with desk lamps taped to the ceiling in place of stage lights, the club where I'd started out eight years previously.

I slowed down and tuned in to hear a man replying, 'Oh right, where is she these days?' I recognised his voice as an Irish comedian, a middle-aged white man with a commercially successful line in 'What are we like at all at all' comedy. I hope that doesn't give him away. At that point, I should have put down my umbrella, turned around and congratulated him on his 17th DVD release, but I didn't. His wife, the lady who had first noticed my name on the blackboard, went on to say, 'She's in London and the last I heard, she was waitressing.' Then the comedian laughed, and so did his wife.

It was probably a laugh of recognition, a laugh that said, *what a funny old business is show*, but in that moment, I didn't hear a kindly chuckle of empathy. I heard two monsters guffawing as they galloped around the empty chambers of my already fragile ego, smashing it to bits.

I felt hot and winded. I ground to a halt as the comedian and his wife jaunted on by, laughter trailing behind them. I ducked into a fancy grocery shop and stood inside the door with tears of fury stinging my eyes. Luckily there was a miniature vegetable display near the door. I always find small versions of things soothing to look at. Absolutely tiny aubergines polished to the depths of their purpleness snuggled next to adorable little courgettes. They were perfect and pretty, but even they didn't make me feel better.

A friend of mine, an unconventional and great man, once went on a business trip to Singapore with three of his straitlaced colleagues. They all stayed in the same hotel and one evening he overheard them having a giant bitching session, poolside. The main subject was my friend – his work, his looks and his personality. He was thrilled. He lay under a low wall to listen to them some more, smoking and trying not to giggle too loudly at what they were saying about him. I know whom I'd rather hang out with. Smokers are cool!

I tried to be more like him. *So what?* I thought, attempting to steady myself. *So what if I used to live in a beautiful house and have my own TV series and then all that fell away and now I live in a terrible flat with a mouse colony under the sink and the only gig I have is right back where I started? So what if I can't afford to buy these fancy vegetables to make a teeny pot of privileged ratatouille? Yes, I've taken a waitressing job in a soulless hipster restaurant in Shoreditch. Yes, the owner does coke in the office and siphons my tips. So what? Since when did I care so much about success and status?* Since I lost them, it seemed, and since others who note such things reminded me of that loss.

I stood there, stock still in the aisles, and retreated into my imagination; always a relief. Along came a comfortingly detailed revenge fantasy. *I'll be back,* I thought, rather hysterically. *I will rule the networks.* Then I remembered two things. One is that Ireland only has three TV channels and the other, crucially, is that I truly don't care about being on TV. But still. How hurtful! I would never gossip about anyone, not in a million years. Justice must be served. *Maybe that lame comedian and his wife will get some rare disease and need a bone marrow transplant and I'll be the only match! Then I'll relish telling them, my voice heavy with irony, 'Oh I'd love to donate but table six need their scrambled gull eggs. Looks like you will have to wait.'* They would have to *wait* – get it?

They say the learning is in the doing. I know that the only way I could learn how to fail was by failing. It's a tricky business, one I was not expecting and one I was having trouble handling with grace. I grew up on stories of bad boys coming good and poor people getting rich and losers finally winning. I love nothing more than a frumpy girl taking off her glasses on the way down the stairs, before walking gracefully into the arms of a stunned and handsome man.

The narrative of my life was not following the anticipated three-act structure, where the heroine was doing fine until she was struck down by some unexpected force. She was in peril, with shadows closing in and then boom! Another twist and she's back on top, maybe even with blonde hair extensions. I was stuck in that second act for a long while, waiting for a happy ending that fogged up and slipped out of view as time went by.

When you're stuck there, it's difficult to talk about it. On chat shows and in real life, people find it so easy to tell the story of how things *were* bad, but that was before. Now, they say, things are great! But what about when things *are* bad? I wondered why I never heard about that. Perhaps people don't tell those stories, until they get to the end. Or maybe they do tell them, maybe they had told me, but I didn't want to listen, because I didn't like how it went. It wasn't like a film at all, no. It was too complicated, too messy and too sad.

Now I will listen. Now I do listen because I understand, like anyone who is awake to the world, that at some point in most lives, things fall apart.

A shop assistant dressed like an Edwardian gentleman snapped me out of my static reverie by tunelessly humming 'The Flight of the Bumblebees' through his handlebar moustache as he arranged sanitised hay around some pristine heirloom tomatoes. I had to leave. I had to get on with things. But how would I do that, exactly? The first step was to stop crying on the miniature cauliflowers. Beyond that, I had no idea.

Bere with Me

My favourite thing to talk about at parties is how much I love solitude. I appear enigmatic and truly comfortable in my own skin when I say it. People become jealous and there is no better vibe at a party than envy. What they don't know is that I mainly say I love solitude because I'm not sure that I do. I needed to to test it out, see if that statement fits. I grew up sharing a room with three of my sisters. I've lived in capital cities all my adult life. My job, for many years now, involves me talking to groups of strangers. After an unhappy year in London, I decided to test this statement out. Do I love solitude? Or was it just a cool thing to say, like saying, 'My acne makes me look young' or, 'Drake is overrated' – other things I have uttered, neither of which I believe.

To be truly alone, I decided to go back to Ireland and rent a house by the sea. Doesn't that sound idyllic? A little cottage along the shoreline … yes, I'd have the housekeeper open it up out of season, and stock it with the finest game terrine and casks of the ripest brandy. I would loll about in the groves with my hounds for the winter, putting on condition, sharpening up my rummy. Then I remembered I was not a duchess or a rap mogul, I was a broke and broken-down clown. Don't you hate that feeling? When you march up to the cashier with a basket full of the finest truffles in all the land and the lady laughs loudly as you attempt credit card after credit card?

I left London and came back to my family home in Cork to tell my worried mother all about my vague plan. Trust me, there is nothing a busy grandmother enjoys more than an aimless 31-year-old showing up with two suitcases and a dismantled desk. 'The thing is, I'm basically totally free,' I told her, and she agreed it was fantastic news as her eyes flickered around the room, wondering where to put me.

She put me in what we call the 'Granny Flat', an extension built onto the house that was never inhabited by an actual granny, unless a number of adult children ricocheting back and forth count as one granny. The main bedroom was occupied by another grown-up sibling taking a break from the nasty ups and downs of reality. So, I got the couch. The couch directly beneath two skylights, one of which was filled almost entirely by a giant moon. The spare quilts and pillows were trapped underneath my brother's never used CD decks that he'd left in the wardrobe as he moved country four times. In true martyr style, I made do with a baby blanket knitted for Syrian refugee babies by a family friend's knitting circle. I thought about cramming a tiny baby hat on too, but they were stuck underneath a framed photo of Michael Collins. The glass had shattered three years previously and I'd meant to replace it, but never got around to it.

Despite saying goodnight to the moon a number of times, I couldn't sleep that night. The cows in the shed behind the house were keening for their calves that had been trotted off to slaughter that morning. As I grew more tired, their lowing took on a metaphorical shimmer. *I hear you sister*, I muttered, *I lost something this past while too – my own molten-eyed calf – my sense of self, it's been hauled off to the abattoir.* From her bed, my sister threw a snow boot from 1996 at me and told me I needed to sort myself out.

That's how I came to be standing on a dock outside Castletownbere two days later, with my brother's old racing bike in one hand and a suitcase full of tinned tomatoes and crackers in the other. These foods, seemingly chosen respectively for their heaviness and breakability, were to see me through six weeks of living alone on Bere Island. I made my way down the slippery jetty with care, onto a tiny car ferry that smelled of petrol. It was drizzling and the water was churning grey, but I was so distracted by the petrol smell, one of my favourites, I didn't notice the less-than-ideal conditions. We lurched across the sea and I unfolded the map I had printed from a friend of a friend who had bought a house on the island and was going to renovate it and rent it out in the summer months.

For now, December, it was bare and empty and all mine for the cost of electricity – around 40 euro. I knew I could totally borrow 40 euro from my little sister so I said yes, please, and the lady who owned the house sent me a key and a map, both of which I held in my freezing blue hand as I stood on the jetty where the ferry had left me. I peered through the gloam of the morning up the hill, trying but failing to make out the little house that would be mine. I dragged my bag along the mossy ground in what I hoped was the right direction.

The map showed that the island is seven miles long and three miles wide. I thought then that it was about half the size of Manhattan, and tried to check that online. There was no reception and I was annoyed about that and more annoyed that the first thing I thought to do when I got to an island to get away from everything was to go online to see what size Manhattan was. I huffed up the hill, leaving my bike at the bottom. I was confident it would not be stolen, because only 200 people live on the island. In any case, the bike was a borderline wreck. It was old and battered, with handles whose leather had worn through to the metal. It was also a bit too big for most people, including myself. As I unlocked the front door to the cottage, I looked around at the empty houses nearby. I wondered how many people live in Manhattan. Millions I guessed, and how did they all fit?

The house was small and cold and plain, exactly as I'd hoped. There was a small hallway with a storage heater that I did not yet know would become an almost romantic attachment. A front room seemed closed off, and I went through to a sitting room with a stout little solid fuel furnace and a rock-hard sofa. At the back, there was a kitchen and a bathroom, cold in that separate way extensions often are. Upstairs, the bedroom had a lilac floor; the only other embellishments were some tiny glass feet, orange ones, glued onto the windowsill, making it look like a fairy had scampered out the window leaving an amber relief behind. Those weird little feet distracted me for a good ten minutes. They put me in mind of those awful pins that people wear, the silver babies' feet, the pins that say, 'I am absolutely not OK with any of you women getting an abortion.' I forgot all of that when I lay on the bed and looked out the window. The small fields led up to a Martello Tower; I could just make it out through the mist and beyond that tower, of course, lay the sea.

I would explore, at once! Right after I found out how many people lived in Manhattan. After half an hour of scrambling around, I discovered that if I climbed onto the windowsill with the tiny feet and then half-knelt, half-perched on the chest of drawers, I could get one little circle of reception on my phone. Not enough to check Twitter or download any attachments, but enough to send casual messages about what a fun time I was having to family, friends and people I'd met once or twice who seemed nice and unemployed and would surely have time for a pithy back and forth.

Whenever I'm asked for an account of my day, even if it's in the most casual and friendly of ways, I panic and I often lie. An acquaintance or a loved one smiles, 'So, what did you get up to today?' and I go blank. I grope around for things that seem, if not impressive, at least useful. Often, I can't recall just how and where the day went. Although I'm not doing anything illicit or even strange, I feel embarrassed and uncomfortable recalling the ways in which I do pass my days. 'I had a meeting and did a lot of admin and went to the opera,' I will say, like some Holden Caulfield/secretary bot I've created to convince people I'm not a lazy daydreamer. This won't do, of course; I'm a grown-up woman.

So, to begin a process of truth-telling that will see me through to an honest future, here, hand-on-heart, is how I passed a typical day on Bere Island.

— *Before breakfast*: The toilet seat is freezing so I hover like a delicate little hummingbird, an unusual little hummingbird with her white butt out, for the shortest time possible.

— *Perhaps at breakfast time*: I have tea and eat rice cakes with peanut butter. I have brought hundreds of rice cakes with me because they are so light. I brought just one jar of peanut butter – to bring more was a risk I couldn't afford to take because it's one of my go-to foods to binge-eat on. I don't want to boast but I can take in a dozen spoons of the stuff in the time it takes to say, 'Watch out, she's in the peanut butter again!' I sit on the sofa and notice that it is very quiet, extremely quiet. I consider how old and how hard the sofa is, and how angry my sister Daisy would be at the sound of my crunching. I laugh out loud at the memory of her storming out of many a family dinner because of everybody's mouth sounds. It gets quiet again when I've finished laughing and eating.

— *After breakfast, I think*: I use rubber gloves and a shovel to clear out the little stove in the sitting room but it's too tricky to get the embers, so I end up using my hands. After a few weeks of cleaning out the fire with my hands they begin to crack and bleed and the soot stains the cracks black. I find a bottle of Apres Sun in the kitchen but it doesn't help. 'That's fair enough – you never promised you would,' I tell the bottle, as I put it back on the shelf. In any case, I'm pleased with my old-man-of-the-sea hands.

— Sometimes, I put the radio on, but it only picks up RTE Radio 1 which features shows hosted almost exclusively by middle-aged men giving their opinions on things. Nice in a way, it's a place for this under-represented group to finally get a word in. I'm always so curious to know how such shy creatures feel. They must always be encouraged to speak their mind, and they must be listened to when they do. Anyway, I often switch it off.

— *The rest of the day, at least as long as it was bright*: Bere Island is a great place for adventures; the sort of place every eight-year-old child dreams of visiting. Well, at least up until the 1980s when we got *Super Mario Brothers* and *Crystal Maze*. There are shipwrecks and smugglers' caves, stony coves and abandoned forts. There are bats and goats, and fish and seals. I take my bike and cycle somewhere new every day. Sometimes, I go full Blyton and bring a flask of tea with me. I clamber and slip all around the island, rarely meeting anyone on my expeditions. Sometimes I leave my bike at the base of a hill and climb up to the Martello Tower at the top. I even climb inside it, where it is dank and thick-walled and kind of a bore. I climb back out. I am my father's daughter, and I just want to be outside.

Here are some of the things I do in my allotted adventure time:

I follow the yellow daubs of paint on the rocks all the way around the shore, gradually heading up the cliffs to where the Ardnakinna lighthouse stands blinking away in the sun. The second time I go to the lighthouse, a huge bull blocks my path. He is just standing there, rust-coloured and unbreakable. He stares at me as if he had asked me a question and is waiting for an answer. I try to remember if I am supposed to run, or is that when you meet a bear? Should I climb a tree? Or is that what you do during a shark attack? No, no, you are supposed to poke a shark's eye. I dither and he grows bored, it feels like a promising first date that I've lost control of. He walks away, snorting with derision.

I rub my eyes like some cartoon city-person when I first see the mast and funnels of the Bardini Reefer coming out of the sea between Bere and the mainland.

The same afternoon I see a huge white cross in the centre of the island and a statue of the Holy Mary near the ferry that glows blue in the night. The glow is from electric light bulbs wrapped around her ceramic head, not from her virginity as previously believed.

I walk the Doonbeg Loop, past the sheep who really don't care who I am or what I'm doing. One day I come across a dead sheep lying in the long grass, her body pecked by birds already. Her dead sheep head faces Sheep's Head bay and I feel pity for her. I remember my uncle telling me that a sheep only costs around 30 euro, so if one gets trapped or lost, some farmers don't worry too much about rescuing them. I recall that part of me was horrified; another part of me thought that 30 euro was a reasonable price to pay for a great prank. When I was back on my feet, financially speaking, I could buy some sheep and put them in unexpected places, like under my parents' bed or in the back of my sister's car.

I get a madness for the land. I'd never wanted to own property, but some grasping mentality comes upon me on Bere. Every broken down cottage I come across I envision myself buying it. I see myself wrapped in stylish woollen shawls with long white hair and wise, twinkling eyes. Instead of writing short funny pieces I will write mythical poetry that everyone will feel guilty for not understanding. I will burn sage and speak Irish but actually be Californian.

Lonehort harbour is so beautiful it gives me a lump in my throat. Across the way from Hungry Hill, it even has its own battery surrounded by a moat. That's right – a moat. An absolutely hilarious selection of goats live on the battery, picking their way around the cannons, looking out at the sea with their yellow eyes like so many lazy soldiers, their ears pulled down like army-issued caps on a cold day.

One day I get the ferry to the mainland to get some shopping. I order a taxi to pick me up on the other side, texting the driver to say I am getting the ferry and will be in at 12.15. I am still operating on London time. As previously discussed, the people of London may be bordering on charmless, but they have a magnificent public transport system. The ferry arrives somewhere close to 12.30 and I apologise to the taxi man. He won't hear of it.

'Sure why would I mind?' he asks me in a scandalised tone. 'Isn't it a beautiful day?' In a café, I eat scampi that burst sweet and briny in my mouth. It is one of those places where you are encouraged to have a slice of apple tart, and I do so happily. My ears burn red as they do when I eat refined flour – two beacons of guilt glowing on either side of my head. As I eat, I notice two elderly parents accompanied by their giant son all staring at me from the only other occupied table. The son is around my age and for some reason, perhaps his tracksuit and the way he keeps gawping over at me, I think he is intellectually disabled. I smile at the family with my special, 'I see you. I see you and I thank you for all you do,' smile, and the son asks me in a thick, and I mean thick, Dublin accent if I am the girl off the telly, specifically, 'the pregnant one off the telly'. I confirm that I am indeed the pregnant one off the telly, and add that my character had lost her baby. I am sorry to resort to my old tricks, but needs must. I am so pleased to get back on the ferry, with its sweet fumes making me light-headed all the way back to the island.

I get so many frights on my time on the island. I step in something I don't expect to step in, I get lost, a seagull flies at me. I'm a regular heroine from a film, except there is no film and I am genuinely spooked, just for a moment. The thing I am most scared of is swimming in the sea. In case you feel the same I have written a nine-step guide for you to follow, read on and you will find it!

— *Around dusk*: I go back to the house and have a shower before it gets too cold. The conditioner falls off the shelf and I say aloud, 'Oh you'll get your turn, buster, don't worry.' This trend – me speaking to inanimate beauty products – doesn't worry me. Giving the conditioner a personality, one of an impatient child, does worry me, but only slightly. One day, the water runs brown and then disappears. I try to find the man who is in charge of water on the island. I go to his house but am turned away by a dog that barks in a 'just doing my job' sort of way. I find the man, he is old, with a woollen cap and a lot of stories. He has turned off the water and forgotten to turn it back on again and assures me he will remedy this. The following day, he does. In the meantime, I fill the kettle with an outside tap belonging to one of the empty houses, and use that for tea. I am filthy with mud and grass and coal dust and I even notice a couple of little sand hoppers in my shoes.

— *Sunset*: It is remiss of anyone to go to Bere Island and not make it their business to cram in as many sunsets as possible. This might seem greedy but it won't even be up to you, your eyes will be pulled west if you're in the vicinity of the sea so you may as well enjoy the show. And it is a show, at times bordering on the flamboyant. Pure 1980s style stage, with pinks and oranges swirling together, the sun a reluctant diva that needs to rest but doesn't want to leave her audience. The sky is so wantonly gorgeous I am almost embarrassed for it.

— When witnessing the majesty of a West Cork sunset, it's impossible to think about who was or was not invited to the party or what to work on next or how things will play out in the end. The height and the water and the air rush through your eyes and lungs and heart, marauding up to your brain shouting the news that none of that matters. I stand there and understand there. I understand that when there is nobody around, I'm nobody. I'm not a daughter or a girlfriend or a comedian, I'm not someone who consistently mispronounces the word 'antibiotics' and forgets to post that card. I don't charm strangers or sell out or tell lies. I'm not Irish or a woman or a writer. I am a creature on a cliff breathing in and out.

— *Before the night cold sets in*: After my shower, I light the fire. I had cleverly brought a firelog with me but it turns out that only serves one fire. The rest are up to me. This is very difficult because I never paid attention all the hundreds of times my parents lit the fires at home. I remember being annoyed at all the rustling noises they made, and the snapping and huffing. Wait a second; were they even lighting fires?

Anyway, it's very difficult and it does not work when I just ball up some old newspaper and put a match to it and then throw some glittering coal on top. The little stove putters out. I understand you must blow gently and use kindling. Again, I am talking about the fire.

One day I relent and go to the little post office and shop on the island. I ask the lady there if she sells turf and she tells me she does, that I can pay her and someone will drop it up to the house later on. I forget to ask her who, and at what time, and how she knows which house I'm in. I'm too distracted by the biscuits I peep on the shelf behind her head. Later that evening a battered old van pulls up the laneway and judders to a stop outside my house. I watch a small boy hop out of the driver's seat and walk around to the back. He yanks open the rusty back door and drags out a bale of peat briquettes. An even smaller boy leans out of the open passenger window; he seems to be instructing the slightly bigger boy on where to leave the bale. I open the front door and shout my thanks. They nod silently as island men do and I could have sworn the toddler tipped his cap before the van trundled off down the darkening hill with no lights on.

— *Dinnertime*: Eating alone leads to all sorts of weirdness. In my defence, I sort of forgot how to cook in London and the food I'd brought to the island was odd in both senses of the word: it was strange and it didn't match. There may have been one particularly grim incident with some mashed turnip and a tin of sardines. I cannot say. Nobody was there to see it. Actually, in the interest of honesty, I'm glad to admit it. I had mashed turnip and sardines for dinner! There have been other times too, you know, that nobody witnessed, where I actually triumphed. I helped a blind man by telling him blue didn't suit him, and allowed a group of boys to laugh at me on the train when I accidentally tried to open the door to the driver's section.

— *Later in the evenings*: My grand scheme is to write after dinner, but that doesn't happen. I find an old stack of *New Yorkers* and read them instead. I flick through long-dead gossip and restaurant reviews from 2006, heralding the arrival of microherbs to Brooklyn. I lie on the spiny couch thinking about nothing until the fire dies out.

— *Bedtime for Gumpins*: Each night I slip into something more comfortable, my imagination. There I stay, lost in other lives until sleep comes.

I sometimes wonder if I should be scared. I am on my own, a woman, my throwing stars are back on the mainland being repointed, there are no police on the island and very limited phone reception. One night I try to get worked up. I imagine a killer sauntering easily through the back door, which I am not at all sure I have locked. I think I should go down to check that door, and maybe pick up a knife while I am at it. A knife I would keep under my pillow and brandish at anyone unlucky enough to come at me. The thing is, though, it is freezing, and I am so sleepy and cosy under the blankets. And I amn't scared. I don't feel any fear while I am here, so that doesn't mean I am brave, it just means I am here.

One night something magical happens with the wind and I have full phone reception for a minute, long enough to read an email asking if I want to do a show at The Irish Arts Center in New York, one show at the end of January. I sit up in bed and decide I'll go and live in New York. I clamber up onto the chest of drawers and reply, saying I will do the show. Then I jump back under the covers and try to get warm again by curling up as small as I can and putting my hands under my arms.

That's the thing about decisions. We are always making them constantly, always doing tiny things that lead us one way or another. That night I thought, *here are some people asking me to come to New York for a show, I think I will do that, and I'll stay on.* It was just an email I answered – it was just one foot in front of the other. That's how things happen, I suppose.

Face Your Fears in
Nine Easy Steps

Here are step-by-step instructions on how to swim in the Atlantic Ocean.

I trust that you, my darling reader, can read between the lines. This was something that scared me for a long time, for reasons I've detailed below. It dawned on me only after writing this that the Atlantic Ocean is the one thing that lies between Ireland and America. I swam to America! I didn't, but I made a start. I took the first few steps toward the thing I was afraid of. I'm sure that you can too. It's not so bad, I promise.

1. First, make sure you remember how to swim. Then put a towel into a plastic bag along with a pair of old running shoes that are so beat up you don't think twice about

sacrificing them to Big Daddy Neptune. Tie your hair up high and put your swimsuit on under your oldest tracksuit.

2. Lock the back door and off you go. Defy anybody with a pulse to ignore its quickening when they see you riding by on this wintry day, one leg of your tracksuit rolled up so you won't get caught in the rusted chain of your brother's giant bike.

3. Keep cycling, breathing hard up the hills – careful down a rutty path with those uncertain brakes, until you get to some kind of cove. You will know where you're supposed to end up. You'll recognise the bank of dark seaweed frowning on the shore. Trudge through this, ignoring the washed-up bottles and crisp packets and the baleful jellyfish parts. Get to the rocky little beach and do not think.

4. Do not think about how cold it is on this December morning. Do not think about being on your own. Just take off your tracksuit. Feel a laugh bubble up at the memory of crazed magazines screeching criticism about women in bikinis. It doesn't even matter. You are so far away now and this is your perfect beach body.

5. While your fingers are not yet frozen, lace up those runners you've had since fifth year, the ones with

Smashing Pumpkins lyrics written on the canvas. They will protect your feet from the sharp rocks underfoot.

6. Disarm the waves with a smile, then watch your legs turn peach and blue as you hesitate on the shore. Notice the colour of the seaweed, it's green and brown like you always knew, but there's a light purple frond there too, swaying underwater, like, *I'm so pretty – I'm the lilac waggler.*

7. Pay no heed to that thick-necked bouncer of a seal who is lying high up on a rock, assessing you in his glassy, lazy way. Nobody is refused admission to Club Sea, so stand your ground. Match your breath to his, calm and counting – one, two, three.

8. Breathe evenly and look towards the horizon. I'm warning you now that all the things there are to be afraid of, real and imagined, will gather and show up – an unbidden, terrifying slideshow. You'll see jagged drop-offs in the seabed, you'll feel your feet tangling desperately with unseen ropes as rogue currents fill your lungs full of brine, you'll picture floating bodies of unknowable creatures brushing against your face … The hysteria will continue until you realise that the thing you're most afraid of is being too afraid to go in.

9. That's when you'll blank your chattering mind and walk into the water, cursing with joy, further and further, until you find yourself swimming, and you don't feel the cold anymore.

'Eight Million Centers
of the Universe'

In my school, the girls used to play a game called 'American Dream' where they held their breath until they passed out. They got in a lot of trouble for it, both respiratory and parental. I never played, preferring instead my 15-year-old self's version of 'American Dream' which was very different. This American dream involved me imagining myself living in New York City, breathing continuously throughout. The dream was a fuzzy thrilled mess I'd stitched together from films and books. Back then, New York was no more real than any fantasy, an abstract place in a glowing future where I'd have ambition, adventures, a bunch of sardonic friends, a series of tragic romances and bagels, lots of bagels.

Now that I've moved here, I'm trying to figure out what

New York actually is, I'm deciding what to believe and learning how to actually be here. My first clue comes from 'Grand Central', a Billy Collins poem printed small on the back of my subway ticket. It begins, 'The city orbits around eight million centers of the universe.' I think, *That's it!* New York is people.

I wander around Battery Park, looking out at the ferries crossing the Hudson to New Jersey. The Statue of Liberty has her back to me but I don't take it personally. I see One World Trade Centre, under construction and obscured by a heavy mist, but still formidable, gigantic. I grow maudlin as I look at all the people on the street and wonder what it was like here the day of the attack. Just then I see an old school friend, walking down Murray Street with her brand new baby. Delighted by the coincidence (I'm speaking for myself, Gemma seemed … confused? Dismayed?) we have tea in her apartment and I admire the baby. She's an extremely cute baby. The only way she could be cuter is if she had big gold hoop earrings on.

I leave Gemma's building and realise that my phone is dead and I don't know how to get to my show. I start to panic, until I remember an old trick my forefathers used – they would take their headphones off and ask other humans for directions. I bundle onto a bus that says 'crosstown' and find a seat beside an old lady who is all wrapped up in a huge pink scarf, chenille. I ask her if the bus will take me to the Village. Her reply is muffled and musical. 'It sure will, baby.'

I wished I was her baby – I'd follow her everywhere and make her cuddle me non-stop. The bus is warm and travels slowly along Eighth Avenue, rocking slightly, making me drowsy. I look out the window as rickety noodle bars give way to solemn court buildings and I think about the last time I was on a bus, back home in Ireland. Not in a misty-eyed way, it was only three weeks ago. It was the bus from Cork to Castletownbere, except it was a Tuesday so the bus only went as far as Glengarriff. I'd asked the driver if there was another bus that would take me the last 30 miles to Castletownbere. That's when he said, Zen-like, 'I am the bus.' Then he recommended hitch-hiking the rest of the way, which I did.

After the show, I go for dinner with the promoter and his friends. We get talking about who is from where. On my right there's a man who looks like he's from Carlow (90s clothes, baffled face), but is actually a Russian Jew. On my left, a charmingly drunk woman who says she's definitely half-Korean and possibly part Native American. Opposite us sits a man from Guyana who's married to a woman from Trinidad, via Japan. I think about where I'm from, Cobh via Carrigtwohill, and I can't help myself from saying aloud, 'This is so cool.' As the words hit the air, I realise how obnoxious I'm being – collecting and commenting on my companions' ethnicity like they are an interesting new coffee blend. The Trinidadian takes it in her stride, and saves me by saying, 'You should meet this guy I dated once, he was Moroccan-Israeli and I mean … wow.' She pops her eyes and makes a hand gesture that suggests she had a great time with him. Her husband rolls his eyes. Lost for words, I high-five her and go back to my salmon, which was, as far as I remember, both Alaskan and Cajun.

Now I am walking in the Upper West Side and hear a seven-year-old zinging a grown up. They are just ahead, carefully picking their way through the icy puddles, the man carrying the boy's schoolbag and a small violin case. Waiting to cross at the lights, the ear-muffed boy says he doesn't feel like practising today. The man replies, 'Well, Jacob, if you wanna be great at something, you have to do it every day.' The child doesn't miss a beat. 'So you wanna be great at babysitting?' The man inhales through his nose. 'I guess so, Jacob, I guess so.'

In a diner on the lower East Side, a waitress tells me, confidently, 'This is New York City – nobody eats solids.' I overhear a girl, arguing loudly on her phone in the 86th Street Wholefoods, end the call by saying, 'I'm a New Yorker, I'm not going to be stupid about nothing.' I meet a friend of a friend, who has offered to give me the low-down on living here. 'As a New York female I can tell you the guys here are hot, sure, but they are soooo lame. They are, like, Lilliputian.'

I understand she means immature, but she's chosen the wrong analogy and I frown. She mistakes my expression as confusion, and clarifies, 'They never grow up.' I tune out and watch a man somehow hold a toddler and two cups of coffee. He's looking for somewhere to sit, and saying, 'This is not working for us, sweetie, no chairs, na-ah.' The child repeats him, 'Na-ah, Papi'. The New York female asks how I plan on approaching the dating scene, as if it's a dangerous animal that's just woken up hungry. I tell her I don't have a plan and, anyway, I've already been asked out. I don't tell her that it was by an intellectually disabled man who called me Curly and asked me loudly and repeatedly to sit beside him on the subway so we could 'talk closer'.

At Grand Central Station I go to the Whispering Gallery – an arch that you whisper into and the sound travels right across the ceiling to the person listening at the corresponding pillar – but I can't properly test it out because I'm on my own. I consider stopping one of the commuters racing by, but I don't know if they'd appreciate my revelations. *I've been ignoring my credit card debt for six years. I don't actually like bagels. I'm never quite sure what is real.*

Instead I look at my subway ticket again, and read the

last lines of the poem. 'Lift up your eyes from the moving hive and you will see time circling under a vault of stars and know just when and where you are.' That's exactly right, you know, because when I look up I see with total clarity that I'm not dreaming, it is now and I am in New York City.

Culture Schlock

Never has a seam of comedy been mined more ruthlessly than, 'the differences between'. The differences between men and women, the differences between black people and white people, the differences between cats and dogs – it is truly hack stuff, utterly boring to me. And yet I find myself here, standing with my quill in my hand, about to use it to knock down that low-hanging fruit. Sometimes that's the juiciest stuff. I'm about to launch into a rather ruthless list of 'the differences between Irish bathrooms and American bathrooms'. Bear with me? You may find it schlocky, but at least you shall see that I am a human being after all – as messy and full of contradictions as any one of you poor slobs. I hope this complexity we share will keep you intrigued, keep you coming back for more. *Who is she?* You'll think, reading faster and faster. *And will she ever start to make sense?*

1. Title

In Ireland we say 'bathroom'. There is a genteel quality to it, a hint of sophisticatication and wealth, like our eunuch is upstairs in said bathroom, drawing us a bath with our favourite oils. People I know with baths only use them to bathe or contain their children and dogs. In my world, grown-ups don't take baths, except for one curious incident when my friend was getting married and her bridesmaid insisted that she have a bath the night before the wedding, complete with soft Celtic music playing in the background and baffled family members shushing each other in the corridor outside.

Another title that is acceptable, if bold, to say in Ireland is 'toilet'. When I'm being real, which is always, I say toilet. 'Where is the toilet?' I demand, challenging my hosts, eyeballing them as I let them in on my not-so-secret plan to totally expel my waste under their roof.

In America, the bathroom is called the 'restroom', inferring a room you go take a little rest in. Far from straining and screaming, you're just having a little sit down. Some quiet time. There are no grunts or plops to be heard, everyone is simply curled up on individual velveteen futons for a couple of minutes, after which they emerge calm and well … rested.

2. Visibility

The most striking thing about JFK airport is not the cops with guns that patrol around the buildings, or the shoddy WiFi service. The most confronting thing is that the toilet cubicle doors have large and inexplicable gaps in them. There is at least an inch-wide gap between the door and its frame! In this new land, there is no such thing as privacy in public. Let me tell you, it's a real 'welcome to America' moment when you step off the plane and head for the restroom feeling like you made it, only to tilt your head to the side and get a vertical cross-section of a shitting woman.

3. Information Sharing

I was washing my hands in the gym restroom when a girl at the sink beside me began winding some sewing thread around a clove of garlic. I recognised her as one of the fitness trainers, a tough little dance instructor with a shaved head and a beautifully intense face. Before I thought it through, I asked her what she was doing. That's how I found out that asking someone what they're doing with thread and garlic is a terrible idea, particularly if they're in the restroom.

She looked right at my dopey face and impatiently, as if she'd said it twenty times already, told me, 'I've been having a strange discharge from down there. The doctor said to use garlic for the odour.' In the achievement I am most proud of in my life to date, I held her gaze and did not allow my face to crumple. 'Oh cool,' I replied. 'Good luck with it.' I smiled emptily as I dried my hands on some paper towels. In the mirror, her elegant eyes followed me right out of the restroom. I went immediately to the stretching area where I put my headphones in, assumed child's pose and turned my music up as loud as it could go.

Be Maeve Yourself

In this city of a thousand cultures, my name is really my only exoticism. I know this because of the varied and rich misspellings that are thrown my way each day. Maide Higgina's laundry is ready for collection. Meev's iced coffee is up. Could Mr Merv Huggins please come through? I don't mind when someone misspells or mispronounces my name, because here it is foreign and it is odd. I've encountered my name through all sorts of filters, and come to like it even more because of that.

— Maeve sounds like mauve, the colour of a depressed lilac. Don't get me wrong, I love *The Color Purple*, especially the part where Oprah pops up in a field of sugar cane and says, 'You should bash Mister's head open and think about heaven later.' However, I do not love the colour mauve. The only place I would voluntarily wear mauve to would be my son's wedding to a person I didn't much like. I would be that passive-aggressive blob in all the photographs, my unsmiling face peeping out from beneath a large off-lavender hat, letting everybody know just how I feel about this debacle. My poor boy!

— Don't you just hate when you move into an apartment and the little girl who lives upstairs has the same name as you? No need to answer that question – I only asked so I could talk about my own experience. Aren't I brazen? Again that was rhetorical. I thought it unlikely in a place like New York that my name twin would be one floor above me yet that is what has happened. It's happening right now. Upstairs Maeve has upset her sister and is being yelled at by their mother. 'Maeve! Why do you have to always do that?' At this point in my life, the disembodied voice of a critical mother is unhelpful. I work from home. Working from home can mean many things: lengthy studies of Action Bronson videos, whole afternoons gazing at the patterns on the floor counting down the hours to my next snack. It also means being alone most of the time, trying to maintain some belief that I'm normal and am not a mad woman who is alone most of the time for no good reason other than her dread of the outside world. That delicate equilibrium is often rocked by sudden shrieks of, 'MAEVE – what have you done now? Say sorry to everyone!' And I'm back to square one.

— Maeve is a Gaelic name meaning 'comedy legend with a cute butt'. It is an unusual name in America. When I introduce myself I have to explain the pronunciation. I tell people, 'It sounds like Steve, except instead of a "st" sound, it's a "ma" sound and instead of an "eve" it's an "ave".' That's a great little conversation starter for cocktail parties and mother-and-baby yoga classes. It distracts people from the fact that I'm drinking three cocktails at once and also that I don't have a baby; I just find that class a lot easier.

— Maeve Binchy is probably the most famous Maeve in the world. I never met her but I felt a sadness when she died because she seemed wise and kind and determined to have fun, and her books all had happy endings.

— Maeve Brennan is the Maeve I think about the most. Her work is top class, brilliant, sly and brave. Despite being gradually eclipsed by addiction and mental illness, she still managed to invent a new style of writing. In her *New Yorker* column 'The Long Winded Lady' she drew a map of New York from moments that were otherwise unseen – a picture of sparkles and horrors, that is a friend and a guide to me now.

— Like any Queen – Victoria, Latifah, Panti Bliss – rumours and myths have grown up around Queen Maeve. Here is what we know for sure, and by that I mean here is what we know from the Internet. Queen Maeve was queen of the West of Ireland and she had a Sheryl Sandberg attitude about gender equality and the pay gap. She wanted to be as rich as her husband, to get her 'man-share'. When she found out that he had one more bull than her she started a war to get her own bull. She got it! Total hero. My life goals are informed by Queen Maeve, a staunch character, a feminist who had a lot of sex with young warriors and is buried standing up, facing her enemies.

— A friend of mine works as a scriptwriter and told me that the name Maeve is popping up more and more in the indie spec scripts she comes across in LA. She predicts that my name will become a name that hipster parents call their children 'in the next five to seven years'. I look forward to 2020, when I will surely meet brand new Maeves, Maeves with honeyed limbs and no inbuilt guilt being urged to eat their chia seeds in the utilitarian café of whatever godforsaken shared workspace I find myself in.

— Anthropology is the study of humans, past and present, building upon knowledge from the social and biological sciences as well as the humanities and physical sciences to attempt an understanding of the full complexity of humanity. Anthropologie is a store that sells a lifestyle idea to those humans it has studied and deemed wealthy and passive enough to want to buy one. They sell clothes and home décor and accessories for women. Women that love, love, *love* to travel but can't because their marketing job keeps them pinned to Manhattan. Women that adore food but don't eat, women with a powerful career but a carefree sensibility, wealthy women that say money is not important.

This idea of a life that they peddle so well is one I detest and desire in equal parts. I am simultaneously furious and full of longing as I walk around the Anthropologie store in Chelsea Market, waiting to go upstairs to the Google offices for my free lunch with my mathematician friend who works there. My eye is drawn to silk blouses in tribal prints that say, 'This is a good girl's blouse – but a good girl with a secret tattoo! But don't worry – it's just a tattoo of a tiny owl!' I finger a chambray dress that cinches in and falls just right, a dress fit for the heroine of a romantic comedy, that scene at the farmers' market when she drops a pineapple on the hero's foot, what a sexy klutz! This $228 skirt covered with miniature French bulldogs surely belongs to me, a true individual who could dreamily lose a whole afternoon in a second-hand bookstore. I mean, come on – my name is written all over these clothes. It is, you know. My name is actually written on the label. The clothes that beguile me and torment me the most with just how close to the aspirational bone they are? They come from, without exception, the 'Maeve' line.

— I hadn't met the man who lives next door to me until he kindly accepted a delivery of birthday flowers on my behalf. When I went to pick them up the following day he seemed on edge. I thanked him and made small talk, wondering slightly at his discomfort but putting it down to my personality. When I got home, I read the card attached to the bouquet. It was from a friend who likes to joke around about being my mother. I enjoy the joke and often speak to her in a baby voice and tell her that I'm scared of various things. Anyway, the rattled florist had misspelled my name, writing 'Maize, you are a big girl now and you must not eat these flowers. You can only drink my milk, love from your mommy.'

I know my neighbour read the card because when we leave our buildings at the same time and he cannot avoid darting past me, he replies to my cheery, 'Hello,' with a mumbled, 'Um, hey Maize.'

Ol' Boxcar Higgins

The New York City subway has 468 stations serving 24 subway lines. That's a lot. A single ticket costs $2.75. That's a lot, too. You can get an unlimited 7-day ticket for $31, or a 30-day one for $113.50. When you're coming out of the turnstile, there are sometimes people waiting to come through that make it known with a gesture or a low word that they would like you to give them a swipe. That's against the rules but my feeling is that if they have asked you to, then they probably need you to. Plus, if you do it they will think you are cool. So naturally, I give swipes away and everybody wins except the rules and, I suppose, society.

The subway is the last place left in the city to escape the Internet. Most people cling to their phones regardless and a lot of the time I do, too. Other times, I embrace this glitch in the cyber world, this pocket of offline space, and I just sit there and leave my mind off, to wander and wonder as it will. So please, Dear One, mind the gaps on this trip aboard my train of thoughts.

— Incidences of petty and not so petty crime were extraordinarily high in New York in the 1980s. The subway was a dangerous place to be. People love to talk about this now; long-time residents of Brooklyn get a real kick out of telling baby hipsters that 25 years ago, if they were getting off at Bed Stuy, they would need to bring an axe with them. An old lady told me that wild dogs would often be seen roaming around the Parkside Ave stop. People got mugged on the trains themselves. Jewellery was snatched from necks, shoes pulled off feet. That has all changed now. The worst thing that's happened to me on the train is when an old lady with loose teeth sat next to me and ate a plum and by some cruel twist of fate I didn't have my headphones with me.

— Remember reading? Well, people still read on the train and though the librarian in you will want to know just what it is that everyone is reading, there is a delicate etiquette to consider. You are allowed to read something stupid over someone's shoulder, like *The New York Post* because that is not private – it's just a crummy version of the news told in easy big letters and gross photos that are designed to attract the eye. That's nobody's fault except everybody's.

You are not, however, allowed to read someone's book. This is because the print is too small and reading it may well necessitate the type of proximity that can lead to law suits. Also, when you get close enough to read someone's book, you may involuntarily get in synch with that stranger's breath and feel panicked and comforted at once.

— Unlike a real book, it is sometimes permissible to read someone else's e-book, particularly if they have made the font super big, in that case they actually want you to! When I'm reading something I'm proud to be reading, I make that font real big. 'Look into my Kindle,' is what I'm really saying, 'and realise how intelligent and fascinating I am. See which parts I have highlighted, which parts I really *get*.'

— 'A crowded subway is no excuse for unlawful sexual conduct.' So goes the announcement, played regularly on the train. It always makes me think, *Is there any excuse for unlawful sexual conduct?*

— Sometimes, very late at night, the train just doesn't come along. There are no announcements and no sign of any explanation, so all you can do is stand on the platform and wait. Phones don't work down there, so the usual distraction techniques are unavailable. Often you're too tired to worry about it, so what happens is you go into a state of suspended animation and time fades away. Eventually another waiting passenger will sigh and walk up the stairs to find another station or catch a night bus home and, after a while, you will too.

— All of my senses are kept busy on the subway. My eyes are checking which platform I need, where the seats are, which ones are the crazy people. My ears are listening for approaching trains at the same time as they are sort of enjoying the busking drummer but also resenting him. And my nose – I can literally smell a rat. My mouth is full of peanut M&Ms and my hands are feeling around for strangers' butts.

— On freezing-cold days everybody wears dark puffy coats and fluffy scarves over their faces so that only their eyes gleam out from under their hoods. When the train comes they become so many subterranean ravens descending on a metal carcass that ends up devouring them.

— It is best not to pick up a baby that doesn't belong to you. Even if the baby is very cute and reaches up to you and you carry her down the steps without thinking. When the mother gets to the bottom of the steps with the empty pram and turns and sees you with her baby she may well gesture to a spot beside her and say flintily, 'You can just put her right there.'

— If a subway carriage is empty, that does not mean it's your lucky day. There is always a reason, and it is never a good one. Something bad is happening or has happened in that carriage, best not to check what that is: I guarantee it will be something that smells unforgettable, and not in a good way. I urge you to follow the herd to the packed carriages on this one.

— 'Showtime! Showtime! Showtime!' is what kids yell to let you know you need to sit back, they are about to break-dance and flex and hold themselves horizontally on poles, and almost kick the fedoras off the dopes on the L train. It's hard not to watch and hard not to be impressed, though most people do a convincing impression of a nonplussed New Yorker. I like the dancers. If I don't have a dollar I give them a clap. Although I know they'd prefer the dollar, it's better than nothing.

— On my way to an audition where the casting director wouldn't shake hands 'because of germs', a man rushed out through the subway doors past me as I stepped into the carriage. Nothing strange there, everyone is in a rush. As I sat down I noticed a slight commotion going on amongst the three other people in the carriage, each sitting separately. 'That guy hit you, man, he hit you straight bang in the head,' said a young guy to a stunned looking man who was rubbing his head. The second man gestured with a wave of the hand that everything was fine and said in a strong Spanish accent, 'No, no, it was a mistake, he just needed to get his bag from there; it's OK, no problem.' A concerned-looking girl who had taken out her headphones chimed in then. 'Are you sure you're alright? It seemed like he really hit you hard.' The Spanish man winced as he smiled and insisted that he was fine, it was a mix-up and the man didn't mean to hit him. Later that night, my roommate told me a man had been shot by the police because he was hitting people with a hammer on the subway and when he got above ground he hit a police officer, too. I told him that I thought maybe that was the same guy from my train. Then we watched an episode of *Sister Wendy's 1000 Masterpieces*.

— Once on a radio show I talked to a handsome scientist who studied bacteria in the subway. He found traces of anthrax and the bubonic plague and was annoyed at how those findings were what made the headlines. He said that being exposed to a wide range of bacteria is actually a great thing for our health. He said he'd happily roll his baby girl around the subway floor 'like sushi'.

— The colours inside the carriages of many trains are straight out of the 1970s – mustards, oranges and browns. Someone on the design team must have been an autumn. Lots of the trains feel old and a bit rickety. They're clunky and noisy and unpredictable. They make me think that America is only hanging on by a thread.

— The light on the B train really flatters my skin tone and I like to look at my hand around the pole all the way up and under Sixth Avenue. I admire my nails if they're done. If they're not, I hide them and instead I look at the scar on my thumb. I cut it wide open in 2011, because I was tired and clumsy from fasting before a photo shoot. Anyone with a tricky relationship with food will recognise the logic in not eating solid food for three days yet insisting on making a lemon tart for someone else. I sway on the way to the Natural History Museum and remember the doctor who stitched up the wound. I was embarrassed and trying to be breezy. I kept up a patter, telling him funny stories about what a klutz I was. Somehow I launched into why I preferred the Atlantic Ocean to the Irish Sea, because it is more dramatic, more romantic. Before I knew it I had started to cry, and he was kind. Handing me a tissue, telling me everything would be fine.

— One time, on a busy 6 train headed uptown, I went to sit down and a small Puerto Rican man in double denim yelled, 'NO,' and pointed out a pool of urine on the seat. 'I'm doing this reluctantly,' he told me. 'When I got on, some dude told me not to sit there so now I feel kinda obliged.' I nodded, appreciating his effort. I tore a sheet from my notebook – glad I had kept up the out-dated practice of carrying paper around. I wrote 'Be Careful', and floated it onto the puddle. There was a general murmur of approval.

— New Yorkers laugh a lot when I insist my subway station is safe, 'because of all the cops there at night time'.

— If you do happen to pick up a baby that doesn't belong to you in the subway, be careful whom you tell that story to. One girl you will mistakenly take for an ally may well fix you with her grey-green eyes and say, 'That probably wasn't the greatest idea.' Even if you counter with, 'It's just that the little baby had her arms outstretched and she wanted to be lifted up sooooo much.' Even if you do an impression of a pleading toddler – one of your strongest and most requested impressions – she won't budge. 'We all want to pick up cute kids, but not all of us act on it.' By 'not all of us', she means her. You will be forced to narrow your own dirt-blue eyes and reach across her, saying with dignity, 'Thank you, Madame, for your lesson in impulse control. Now if you'll just lean back I need that last little piece of fruit tart from the table.'

— Passengers on a packed Q train to Coney Island that
   stalls between stations at 1.30am on a Tuesday send up
   a sigh so unified and so tired it becomes clear that we are
   all the same and we all want the same thing, and that is
   to get home.

A Man in Full Ownership
of His Basic Sexiness

The day I return to America from a visit to Ireland, I try to have a show in my diary. This makes me feel like I live here and helps take the sting out of leaving Ireland.

The trip from Dublin to New York can take as little as five hours, and the time difference is five hours, so a spooky thing can and sometimes does happen where you arrive here in New York at the same time you left Dublin. Not spooky if you understand flight and time, of course, but I don't. I could learn, but I choose instead to marvel. *This makes no sense! It is magic that I cannot and will not ever get to the bottom of.* I like the magic idea because it makes me feel like there is some stardust on me after every transatlantic flight. I have certainly cheated the clock, gotten some extra hours. Granted, I used those hours to eat shrink-wrapped cheese on a curiously cold bread roll and weep quietly at *27 Dresses*, but still! The afterglow lingers until I break the spell with sleep. I like to bring that hazy feeling with me to shows, like some kind of invisible shield.

One freezing March night, I flew into JFK airport and immediately started the long train journey through Brooklyn and Manhattan to McLean Avenue in Yonkers. I had been invited to an event – no ordinary event, this was 'The Irish Bachelor of the Year' competition and I was a judge. I was a judge! When I first received the invitation I thought – *Who am I to judge? Do we not all have our good and our bad sides, what is this world without light and shade? I cannot decide between these men, are they not humanity itself?* These thoughts lasted maybe 20 seconds, until I remembered that I love to judge and do so unbidden every instant of the day. I judge when it's safe to cross the street, how many eggs are acceptable to eat in one sitting, which one of those firemen would make a cute baby daddy, it never ends! I do not have the connections or discipline or inclination to be an actual judge, a court of law judge, but judging a group of men? That I could do.

Please let me explain to all of you who may feel defensive out there – this was not a beauty contest. Nobody would be checking the men's teeth or making them wear a bikini. The contest did not set out to objectify men. The rules stated that 'The winning bachelor should display certain attributes such as authenticity, charm, politeness, savvy, sensibility and also have an element of fun about them.' And it was all for a good cause: The Aisling Irish Community Centre, a much loved community centre in Yonkers that provides services for Irish immigrants and looks after elderly Irish people living in the city. Surely that's worth going topless for, am I right, fellas?

I was the last judge to arrive and the director, a warm and glamorous woman, gave me a quick tour of the centre. I saw where they serve meals and organise social activities for older people and print CVs and provide citizens' information for younger Irish immigrants. 'Blah, blah, blah; get on with it!' I shouted. 'Show me the men!' Frightened, the woman opened a door to a boardroom and in I stalked. The men, and boys, were milling around a crate of beer. There was a low murmuring of mainly Irish accents punctuated by shouts of loud, nervous laughter. Some of the men were dressed in in their best shirts and ironed jeans, others in the shiniest tuxedos I had ever seen. I smiled and said, 'Hello,' but the hunks were bashful. The director explained how the night would work. The judges would interview each bachelor here at the centre, then we would all travel up to Gaelic Park in The Bronx, where the bachelors would be interviewed on stage and given time to perform their party pieces in the dancehall of the pub there.

I yawned loudly at the mention of the GAA – not because

I was bored, but because my body was still on Irish time. Many of the bachelors caught my yawn, one even yawned in response. It was coming up to 1am in my body, but in Yonkers, the night was young. Choosing a winner was going to be difficult. I knew that instinctively as I stood in that room and watched the little crowd of Irishmen eat crisps and blush furiously. I'd hoped for an instant stand out, a man in full ownership of his basic sexiness. There wasn't one. So I'd have to judge them on the criteria listed. If only I could remember what that was. I spoke to the men, kindly, I promised not to go too hard on them. I reminded them all that I appreciated their efforts – volunteering their time and bodies for a great cause with their only reward a potential title. Then I slowly trailed my fingers across their quivering torsos and left the room.

I was led into a long, narrow office and seated behind a table with the other four judges. There was a Jackie Collins type lady representing the drink sponsors, an efficient blonde lady who emphasised how good the men were to take part, a worried older man and a fellow called John from Cork who seemed mystified as to what was going on and why he was there. The interview process was fun because we were allowed to ask these poor creatures anything! The first contestant was a PE and religion teacher who described his ideal partner as 'female'. I had no questions for him. Others were more interesting. One man lived in lodgings with an old Irish couple and the woman of the house made him dinner each evening. Another man hadn't been home in 12 years and had never met his youngest sister. There was the baby footballer, the gay waiter and a depressed bartender who had spent two years picking fruit in Australia after a bad break-up. There was a local news TV producer and a car salesman. Nobody stood out in the interview process except a Polish man, but that was by virtue of him being Polish. A couple of the bachelors were American, with some Irish heritage. The rest were Irish. I'm sure they weren't all from Cavan, but it seemed that way on the night.

The next step was to get to Gaelic Park, a place I had never visited, a fact that my fellow judges were horrified to hear. 'Not even to see a Cork match?' asked John. No, I said, and added that I'd never seen a Cork match in Ireland either, which chilled the temperature of the cab. I often lose in games of 'Who Is the Best Irish Person Abroad?' and it doesn't bother me. We arrived at the stadium with its low-slung pub out front. Out of the car, the cold night air sharpened me up and I realised I had been drifting along on that magical jet lag and hadn't been paying attention to which films the bachelors listed as their favourites to watch with a girl. I was still no closer to choosing a winner. The haziness I'd been feeling left me completely once I walked into the venue. There was a long bar with a huge dancehall at the back that was heaving with people wearing county jerseys and holding two pints each. There was steam rising off the crowd on the dance floor as the band played loud trad tunes and people held their posters and flags aloft. Each bachelor represented a bar or a social group and they all had a fan club. Everyone cheered and clapped when the MC took to the stage and announced that the competition would begin. We judges sat at a table close to the stage, like a TV talent show but a thousand times better, because this event was raising money for old people's dinners and free advice on how to see a dentist when you're an illegal immigrant.

That's what I kept telling myself as the performances wore on. One young man rapped. Another sang a U2 song. A bouncer and marketing analyst, a gigantic bald man had impressed me during his interview with his passion for yoga. I hoped he might do a few *asanas* onstage because watching a large person be graceful in movement is truly a joy to behold. He didn't do yoga though. Instead, he produced a cowbell and explained that he didn't know how to play it but thought it would be fun to try. The band joined in, two bearded men with guitar, drums and the completely blank faces of people who have provided drinking music for a hundred hasty weddings. I could not tell whether they were enjoying the night or they wanted to die; I wasn't sure myself. *How did I get here?* I wondered dreamily, exhaustion seeping into my bones and filling up my brain. *I thought*

I flew away from Ireland but I somehow landed deeper into Ireland than I've ever been, a bachelor competition in a GAA hall and a man playing a cowbell.

In times of duress, the ladies' room is a safe space to run to between the bar and the dance floor. A quick trip there is a moment away from the madness, a chance to unbutton those skinny jeans and give your head as well as your butt some breathing space. Ladies' rooms are for checking your eyeliner, emptying your bladder and making decisions in a relatively calm environment. That was just what I needed, so I wriggled through the nylon GAA jerseys and fake tans toward the blessed door marked with the patron saint of piddles, that little stick figure in a skirt. She beckoned me toward relief, but when I pushed the door open I found a hot new mess. There was a broken pipe flooding the floor, one girl vomiting into the sink in a Roscommon accent and two girls arguing with each other, again in a Roscommon accent. My frazzled mind whirred, trying to make sense of it all; I spun around, searching for the door with all the melodrama of a fragile Hitchcock heroine. How had the door to the ladies' room become a portal to hell?

I found my way out and pushed through the crowd who had swarmed closer to the stage and were hooting with something like joy, something like panic. Some were chanting, 'Get, It, Off'. I got back to my seat just in time to see the melancholy fruit-picker rip off his tuxedo, revealing a long winter of neglect clad in a sparkling red thong. The crowd couldn't settle after that, but I could. A sort of stoned peace came over me as the night wore on. I floated benignly amongst the sweating, cheering audience and looked passively on as the red-faced bachelors drank to drown their self-consciousness and actually speak on stage. The host asked one bachelor, a stout and smiley waiter, how he would sweep a lady off her feet. The waiter replied that he didn't know, in fact *he* wanted to be swept off *his* feet. Probably better than a previous contestant's response: 'I'd give her a good kick to the knees,' but as I say, I was at Zen-level chill so neither statement truly registered with me.

This waiter was the same man who had named Celine Dion as the person he most admired. During his interview he had made two strong arguments for his right to win: one was that he was the only gay man in the competition and the second was that he was a great dancer. 'I moved to New York with dreams of Broadway and ended up tending a bar on McLean Avenue,' he told us, clapping his chunky little thigh and laughing loudly to banish the pathos. His high-energy re-enactment of the 'All the Single Ladies' dance raised the roof of Gaelic Park, despite the fact that he didn't know the steps.

I don't mind, I thought, smiling and clapping. *I don't mind what happens because nothing even matters.* I was drifting now, the contestants blurring before me. As a party piece, one of the bachelors chose 'to tell a few jokes'. I don't remember what the jokes were, but they involved sexual humiliation, high levels of shame and a mouthful of beer dribbled down his shirt as a punch line. Had I not been so spaced out, I would have protested at him stealing my act.

My esteemed colleagues led me to our judges' chambers: a small storage room with a desk covered in invoices and stacks of cardboard boxes filled with bottles of spirits. Joan Crawford looked pleased. I perched on a keg and said that they all deserved to win. The blonde lady frowned and urged us all to discuss it thoroughly. And we did; I was there, physically, and we talked for so long that the barman came in and warned us, 'This crowd won't hold for much longer.' I have no memory of what was said, but I know that the dancing waiter won the title, becoming the official 'Bachelor of the Year 2014' much to the delight of the assembly.

Everyone, including the other contestants, cheered and danced as though they themselves had won. A conga line may have started, swerving around the spilled pints and shattered glass. I really don't recall. You see I wasn't actually there, I was someplace over the Atlantic Ocean, halfway between Ireland and America, wondering which direction would take me home.

Talk Closer to Me

A dull man at a party once asked me what the dating scene is like in Dublin. I hesitated. How can you explain a crazed witch's shimmering mirage? What is there to say about a ghost you have only heard of, a ghost whose shadow you can only snatch at? I knew that if I tried to explain 'the dating scene in Dublin', I'd be stuck with the man all night because there is no quick way of explaining the complex mating rituals of Dubliners, that subtle dance that nobody quite knows the steps to. How could I make that clear to this glassy-eyed cypher in front of me?

I decided I couldn't. Instead, I said, 'The dating scene in Dublin is like the jungle and the women are the big cats. Now if you'll excuse me, I've just spotted an impala that's been separated from the herd.' Then I sprang away from him toward a nervous looking writer type – knock-kneed, wide-eyed, easy prey.

I know a man who was once a contestant on a game show called *Take Me Out*. Like many Irish versions of international TV shows, there was a peculiar poignancy to the show. The production company couldn't afford to send the winning couples on an actual date. Instead, the winners just walked from the stage down some illuminated steps to the backstage area. There they sat on a scratchy-looking couch for 20 minutes. and chatted, the women heavily made-up, in cheap dresses, the men pale under the lights and jittery under the pressure. Seán said it was good craic, but he wouldn't do it again. A week after the show, one of the contestants emailed him asking if he'd like to get a drink with her. He was appalled as he told me about it, shaking his head, 'I mean, talk about *forward*.'

Sex is where the magnificent silence of the Irish comes into its own. In our teens, we enter into an unspoken pact of indirectness and we stay right there as we muddle through our 20s and haul ourselves on up to our 30s. Getting together invokes a 'don't ask, don't tell' code. Hell breaks loose when some poor innocent gets a bang on the head and breaks that code by stopping to inquire of their opposite number, 'Can I just check what this is – like, what *we* are?'

Once they utter the question, the skies are pulled down upon them, forest animals run shrieking for higher ground, clocks melt in shame. An elderly Cupid appears in a puff of furious smoke. Gouty and grumpy he booms, 'You spoke those words and the magic stopped. You dragged this perfectly risk-free encounter into something like reality. Yes, you were just trying to save time, but you broke the rules!' Then he tightens his bow with his fat, tobacco-stained fingers and points his arrow, not at their lover's heart, but right between their eyes. Twang! They're dead.

There is no such thing as dating in Ireland. Naturally, people go for drinks. They most certainly do go for drinks, bravely and quietly marching to the pub; these valiant men and women are in the trenches and like all good soldiers they do not dare to question the reasons behind the battles they fight every day. Those drinks could mean anything: a friendly hello, a networking opportunity or maybe, whisper it now, a romantic connection.

Questions swirl around both parties' heads, questions like – *are you gay? Is there someone keeping a dinner for you? Do you fancy me? Is there a smaller someone who looks like a miniature mixed-up version of you and another someone? Do I even fancy you?* These questions never make it out of our mouths. We keep quiet and we keep circling, until the cold or the alcohol drives us together.

And even after doing it and doing it and doing it well, the mystery remains. *Are we … together? Is that … my boyfriend?* Silence! The only way you know for sure that you're officially in a relationship with someone is when you buy a house together. The accrual of joint debt is the strongest evidence of togetherness you can hope for. A wedding will probably come along too; these unions are, in their own way, arranged marriages. Instead of concerned parents doing the arranging, it's geography and vodka.

Stephen King wrote the short story 'Crouch End' based on his visit to that part of North London. The legend goes that after asking for a good place to walk, he was directed towards the old railway line and was inspired by the strange and unsettling surroundings he found himself in. There is a sculpture of a Spriggan, a Pan-like green creature, pushing its way out of an old arched wall that particularly seems to have really stuck with him. I thought about Stephen King with his dear old square head and giant glasses as I got on the bus to Crouch End for a date. *Maybe this will be MY first real horror story,* I told myself excitedly. *Maybe this guy will be a bad-tempered little demon man! And he'll make me promise him something I cannot deliver and a promise to a Spriggan is binding so then I'll have to kill myself or he'll steal my nephews and put boring, sickly children in their place!* I was so lost in thought I missed my stop on the bus. Then, of course, I had to compose a text to my sister that didn't make me sound crazy but did insist that she make sure her children were not changelings. I was 20 minutes late as I walked into the pub, smiling brightly.

Turned out my date was not a Spriggan but an adult

human male who was fully aware of and accepting of the fact that he was on a date. These were indeed strange and unsettling surroundings. I was on edge, when suddenly a dog, a spaniel, rested his head on the arm of my chair and sighed loudly the way dogs do. I forgot that dogs are allowed in pubs in London. For a few terrifying seconds I thought a silky-faced, floppy-eared woodland spirit had come out of the wall and rested its brazen head beside me. I jumped out of the chair, not screaming exactly, but almost.

As you can imagine, my hysteria threw off the rhythm of the evening. I had interrupted my date's most moving monologue thus far – a long piece about when he was in Ireland on a book tour and experienced 'Irish time' first hand. I tried to get things back on track by shoving the spaniel's face away, then asking what he (the man, not the dog) meant by 'Irish time'. He explained patiently in his cut-glass English accent, 'Irish time is when people take a long time meandering around a topic instead of just getting to the point.' I replied, swiftly and efficiently, that I had lived in Ireland most of my life and had not experienced this phenomenon. I asked him for an example and he told me about a woman in a sweet shop who told him 'practically her entire life story' before serving him.

I wondered how busy he was that he had time to visit a sweet shop at all. A quick dash for a scoop of clove rocks and a bag of chocolate mice before continuing on his way to conquer the world of literature – held up by a terrible old lady who didn't appreciate the urgency of his mission. Naturally, I took my sweet Irish time before seeing him again. Perhaps I could have forgiven him his ignorance if everything else had been in order. It is completely acceptable to forgive slight racial slurs if they are

a. against your own people, or
b. uttered by someone you are attracted to.

However, there was no chemistry, no physics and certainly no biology between Little Lord Fauntleroy and myself, so I stayed up on my Crouch End high horse, completely alone, tut-tutting into the night.

The idea of two adults openly assessing each other on the grounds of attraction and suitability is even more acceptable in New York than in London. In this blessed new world deals are struck and negotiations entered into without shame or confusion, and nobody blushes except me. Here is a recent exchange between people that I transcribed as faithfully as I could, once I got my bearings. It happened in a bar in the West Village.

Adult 1: We should have a drink, would you like to go out?

Adult 2: Totally, let's do that. How's your week looking? I could do Thursday after 7pm.

Adult 3 (me): What? Oh my God like I can't believe this what the fuck it's so simple and this whole time oh Jesus what have I been doing I want to start over how is this possible it's no big deal just be honest and direct and say what you want but then how has the Irish race even continued on some level these people are so clinical but no no it's not like what we do is in any way romantic they are right and I am wrong oh what will become of us all?

Adult 1: Ma'am, do you need us to call someone?

Three days after I arrived in the city I got asked out. I was on the subway and I heard a man shouting, 'Come here, Curly!' Curly is my favourite of The Three Stooges, so I looked around hopefully before realising that Curly had surely passed on to that great mime bar in the sky. I was picturing a cross-eyed angel with a balloon tied to his jacket when I was brought back down to earth, under the earth in fact, back onto the Q train as it shunted toward Brooklyn. The shouting man was louder now. 'Come here, Curly in the black – talk closer to me.' There could be no doubt about whom he was addressing.

My hair is part wavy, part curly, part frizzy and a little bit straight underneath. To the untrained or male eye it appears, simply, 'curly'. That very morning I had described my outfit to my sleepy roommate as 'a ninja's widow who works as a bouncer'. That's right – all black. And of course the Romeo was talking to me! I am, after all, *me*. Bashful, I pretended not to hear, but like any romantic hero, the man was persistent. He clapped twice and yelled at me again, 'Curly in black, I like you. Come here and talk closer.' I liked him too, with his sideways baseball cap and dirty overalls, but not in the same way.

In New York, catcalls on the streets are as common as rats on the tracks. That said, the first time I was catcalled I was surprised, for two reasons.

The first was that I had never been catcalled before – men rarely catcall women in Ireland because of the high chance that they are related to that woman. A man who takes the time to look at a woman's face after a catcall may well realise he has just told his niece to take care of that ass.

The second reason I was surprised was that it was a freezing February day and I was bundled up in all the clothes and coats I owned. I looked like a lumpy tower of dumplings wrapped in a quilt. The sleet was stinging down as I battled along Third Avenue, my entire head obscured by my broken-winged umbrella. I was lamenting my missing mittens when a jeep stalled in the heavy rush-hour traffic and the driver shouted something to me.

Assuming he needed directions, I yelled, 'What was that?' and took my earphones out slowly, fingers stiff from the cold. He repeated himself twice, looking more annoyed each time until I finally understood him. 'I'm sayin' you're beautiful, that's all!' he shouted crossly, before speeding on, the cars behind him honking. I broke into an astonished laugh. My bright red hands wrestling with the umbrella were the only clue he could have had that I was even female. Despite that, he still felt the need to halt a busy lane of traffic and let me know what was on his mind.

Had he stuck around, I could have told him that I didn't want to be assessed by him, that I didn't need his approval, that what I look like is not something I want to think about whenever a man feels like bringing it up. I could have also asked him if he had a functioning umbrella to protect my beauty from the elements but, like I said, he did his duty and was gone.

When it comes to catcalling, many men seem to be calling a cat that they don't particularly expect to find, but feel they should look for anyway. They're a little bored as they trawl the streets, doing this job that nobody asked them to do. One man, lying on his side watching a baseball game in the park, called lazily over his sloping shoulder as I jogged past, 'Why don't you run to me, Mami?' I didn't have the lung capacity to explain that I was actually going for a run, and running ten foot towards him then stopping would defeat the purpose of said run.

Others make more effort, like the scrawny man who was

breaking up boxes at my local supermarket and paused as I passed by, making a sound like a baby who's just tasted something hot. 'Oooh,' he cried, crumpling up his face, 'Eeee – aye – *caliente*.' I set my face to 'stern deaf girl' – brows down, mouth tight. He shouted something at me then, crossly, in Spanish. I didn't understand it but it was clear that he was annoyed that I didn't respond more positively to his initial sounds. It's a tedious cycle: man wrongly believes he is complimenting woman who is angered, thereby angering him, thereby angering her even more, until everyone is angry and so on and so forth.

Right now the way I deal with catcalls is the same way I deal with everything that happens in my life – I act like nothing is happening and then, later, I write about it in my room. This clever technique cannot last forever and one day I plan on taking some action. Michel de Montaigne says that the most certain sign of wisdom is cheerfulness, and I believe him. So I need to figure out how to deal with this phenomenon in a good-natured way.

Perhaps the aggressive, sexual catcalls – where a guy mutters as he walks past that I should suck his dick – could be met with a polite, 'Oh thank you, but I'd better not, I've just eaten.' What about when they suggest a more involved position, like a bandana-wearing man did as he left the DNA testing centre around the corner from my house? The centre has a large sign out front, it's a picture of a cute baby with sparkling blue eyes and a question in large font asking – 'Does he really have your eyes?' Maybe I should have responded with honest specifics to this particular man's request. 'I'll tell you now – I slipped a disc in my back a few years ago, well not so much slipped rather it bulged, but it still bothers me from time to time, particularly when I bend over. So that particular position is probably not ideal for me, but thank you so much for thinking of me and have a lovely day and is that your son in the stroller? Oh you're not sure? Well, in any case, he is adorable!'

Not all catcalls are sexual in nature. My favorite catcaller dawdles outside my local bodega and is exclusively in the business of stating sartorial facts. I walk past in a blue dress and he hisses, 'Girl, you got dat blue dress on.' All I can do is agree. When I have time, I'll join him for an afternoon and we can both stand around, happily pointing out things around us. I might say, 'The child is eating ice-cream and wearing a pink romper,' and he will fist-bump me delightedly before yelling at a pastor, 'I see your brown shoes, brother.' We will be two friends on the corner, describing the outfits of people passing by.

That happy future is possible of course, but first I had to deal with this man on the train, the one who'd christened me Curly and was insisting that I 'talk closer' to him. The carriage was packed and many people were doing those little tight public transport smiles, so I knew they were listening.

I wasn't sure how to proceed, because the man seemed to be intellectually disabled. I'm not just saying that because he liked me: there were other clues too. I couldn't shut him down harshly because that would be cruel, and what if he had a sexy carer nearby who was eavesdropping? If there's one thing hot guys go for in a woman, it's a kind heart.

'No thank you,' I said. 'I need to stay right here because my dad is coming.' I don't know why I said that. Freud would probably take a guess. In any case, the man in the dirty overalls bought it. 'OK,' he said. 'I'm gonna wait until my stop which is DeKalb.' I replied, 'OK,' and smiled at two teenage girls who were openly laughing at the man. They didn't smile back, turns out they were laughing at me too, so I quickly changed my smile to a glare.

Further shattering the myth that people don't talk to one another on public transport, a middle-aged woman in a pant-suit asked me if I was Irish. I said I was and she nodded, pleased. 'That's why he likes you – your accent.' I told her that he had started talking to me before I had opened my mouth, but there was no going back, she was off. 'I love Irish guys!' She leaned toward me. 'That accent, my God, talk about a panty dropper!' I winced as she continued. 'Oh my God, whenever an Irish guy opens his mouth I'm like, please, take me right now!'

I explained that it's different when that accent is coming from your brother, or the elderly man with the racking cough who delivers the coal, but the lady was not for turning. I told her she should move to Dublin and give the dating scene there a whirl. She said she'd seriously think about it. I didn't have time to warn her about the pitfalls before she got off at DeKalb Avenue. As she walked up the platform I saw the man in overalls catch up with her and ask her something. I couldn't make out what he said over the noise of the closing doors, but she laughed luxuriously before turning to wave to me.

Find and Keep
Your Mr Wonderful

Here are some wonderful man-getting tips for straight girls and gay guys, with insincere apologies to straight guys – these tips aren't for you. Don't complain – you get everything else!

1. Break the ice

The initial approach can be difficult, what is there to talk about? Think carefully – do you have anything in common? Start small – check if he has eyebrows. If he definitely does, you could say, 'I beg your pardon, but what are those things? Those thin/thick lines of hair over your eyes? I've got them too, see? Always wondered about them.' Then waggle yours, but not too suggestively – you don't want to give him the wrong idea. You just want to launch yourselves into a discussion on eyebrows. He might say, 'How strange they seem, when you take the time to look!' The great thing about you two having something in common is that the guy will take it as a sign that you should be together. Straight guys are constantly reading into things. They don't believe in coincidences. When they see a fruit delivery truck with their name on it or hear the same song from a 1990s TV show played twice in one day *in different shops*, they text their friends excitedly, saying, 'What is the universe trying to tell me??'

2. Go big or go home alone forever

Straight guys love a girl who is not afraid to commit. So when you see your Mr Wonderful and you're sure he's the ideal partner for you, resist the urge to introduce yourself. Instead, covertly take photos of his tattoos, placing your selfie stick at a subtle angle. Alternatively, get his mug shot from the public record. Pop the images into your bum-bag and make your way down to your local tattoo parlour and ask for the *exact* same tattoos – using the photos as your guide. After you've removed the cling-film and they've scabbed up nicely, simply find that cutie again. Bitter experience and the scarring from my expensive painful laser surgery reminds me to always find out where he lives *before* I rush to get inked.

Now comes the fun part. Let yourself be seen. Isn't that

a wonderful thing? I wish I could hold your face as I tell you to *let him see you.* That said, don't just march up there, brandishing your forearm. Play it cool, reach across him in the coffee shop, pretending you need soy milk. He'll likely be surprised, so bear with him while he pales and stutters, 'But but – that's Moms – why you got my mom's face on your arm?' That's when everything you've learned in your 2004 'Free Introduction to Film Acting' class comes into play. Act surprised, tell him you don't understand what he means – you simply have a tattoo of a tired-looking woman and some random dates on your little arm. Tell him you need to get going, and as you turn your head he will see the little swastika you have on the nape of your neck that matches his. This guy you've chosen is a real bad boy! Be that as it may, he will surely call you back – back to his table or back to his cell. Back to your brand-new life together, back to your destiny.

3. Do the work

We've all spent time studying, right? I'm sure you've wiled away plenty of days and nights studying sciences, languages, even the arts (whatever that means!). Well congratulations, Professor Lonely, you've been wasting your time. Unlike you, my wall is not crowded with qualifications and my head is not cluttered with in-depth knowledge of any particular subject. And still, I'm a world authority, because I have spent my time studying guys. I absolutely mesmerise guys. I mean, not mesmerise, *memorise*. I memorise guys, you know, by studying them. I ask questions and I find answers. Are they an autumn? Yes. So I buy them a moss green turtleneck. Do they take sugar? What type of sugar? Do they stir it into their coffee or do they just eat it in handfuls from the bag? Pay attention.

Get your nose out of the books and keep your eyes on your target! If you happen to fall for a non-English speaker, then figure out which funny language they do speak. That's the only exception to the 'no learning anything else except guys' rule. Learn their language, or at least the basic phrases needed to keep a long-term relationship functional and fun. I know how to say, 'Would you like some money?' And, 'Please please stay by my side – just for this party.' In Afrikaans, Portugese and modern standard Urdu.

4. Enjoy yourself

Sometimes, you must put your personal enjoyment actually ahead of the guy you own. 'Own' is probably the wrong word – let's say, ahead of the guy you're 'with' (but we all know what I mean). Put *you* first, before the guy. Doesn't that sound odd? It certainly does to me! However, based on anecdotal evidence collected from long conversations with Alain de Botton, it's the truth. Not the chatty middle-aged TV philosopher Alain de Botton. My source is Alain de Botton, the chatty middle-aged tree surgeon I met online then in real life at a Baskin Robbins. I say middle-aged, this guy was actually only 28 years old, but he is a morbidly obese chain smoker and with a job like his involving chainsaws and heights? I'm guessing he's at his own special middle age right now. Alain told me, between delicate spoons of a cookie dough sundae, that he loves nothing more than a partner who knows how to have a great time in bed. So don't be afraid to go with what your body wants – perhaps that's curling up into a tiny ball and humming tunelessly as you watch the *30 Rock* episode where Liz Lemon sits beside Oprah on a flight for the sixth time in a row. Or maybe it's lying face-down in a star shape listening to long-form journalists being interviewed about their process, as your heart rate gradually becomes slow and even? Whatever it takes, enjoy yourself – because in some rare cases, like big fat Botton's, that is guaranteed to D.H.W. (drive him wild).

5. Be sassy

In the documentary *Seven Brides for Seven Brothers*, Howard Keel rides into town determined to find a wife. He provides women and girls (yawn – heteronormative Wild West!) with a handy checklist for what men want. He wants his girl to have 'heavenly eyes' and be 'just the right size'. The first one is easy – do a smoky eye in greys if you have brown eyes or browns if you have blue eyes. The size thing varies from culture to culture. Here in the actual West you can check the *Mail Online* for a steer on what you should look like, they constantly monitor women's bodies – like the Taliban, just with more celebrity photos. Keel sings that his girl must also possess a particular attitude, specifically, 'as sassy as can be!' So, be sassy. I think that involves having opinions, but I could be wrong.

6. Communicate

You might feel exhausted or grumpy but you must put on your brightest smile and you must chatter. Keep chattering until the break of dawn, because communication is key. I cannot say what it is key to, but it is certainly *key*. So, ask him questions about anything that crosses your mind. No figarie is too slight. Involve him in your struggles. Does this milk smell gone off? On the turn, perhaps? If a dreaded silence does descend and you find yourself without words, please stay present. Never, ever let him forget that you are in the room. If he's not looking at or snuggling with you, dominate his consciousness in other ways. Make tiny little sounds. Peel your nails. Clear your throat, in a delicate way. Do not make a guttural sort of wrenching sound. Guys hate that.

Actual Goddesses Rediscover What It Is That They Truly Want and Need

If you're laying in bed next to someone who really doesn't make you feel like the goddess that you are, you need to rediscover what it is that you truly want and need.
Lady Gaga

1. I am Baubo. Sure, I fudged my age in my profile. And yes, maybe I sent in a slightly misleading photo taken from a height where you couldn't tell that I was actually a naked headless torso with my face in the centre of my body and my vulva in the chin of my face. But everybody's gotta

get theirs and I knew you wouldn't swipe right if you saw the real me. But we had fun, right? I mean, who else is going to show up to the club on the back of a boar, holding a goddamn harp? Not those toothpick kids you're used to dating, that's for sure. I'm *so* sorry you are threatened by my sexuality. I hope you picked up on my tone right there. I am being sarcastic. Us crones are good at that. In fact, I'm good at a lot of things – as you found out. YES I MEAN SEX. And I can turn a bad situation around in a heartbeat. You know when Persephone got dragged to the underworld and her mother was freaking out? I'm the one who cheered her up! I can literally cure depression. I'll brighten your day, boy, I'll make you laugh. If you don't need that then you just keep on walking. No shade, brother, but I'll keep my chin up.

2. I am Sekhmet – one of the oldest deities of Ancient Egypt. A lot of people find that interesting, but not you. You just wanted to talk about your novel. The one you have yet to write! Do you know how tiresome it is for a woman to listen to a man talking about the art he hopes to create? I'm sure you don't. Just like you don't know that my main job is Goddess of War and Destruction but I have a sideline in healing. How could you know? You didn't ask me one question about myself! You complimented my mane and then proceeded to fuss

about whether or not you should do an MFA. Come on, you're dealing with the Lady of Slaughter here, the Mistress of Dread. Surely the serpent coiled around my lioness head gave you some inkling as to what I do all day, every day. I heard all about you, of course. How you're hoping to learn Spanish, how you have stayed friends with all your exes. Your pontifications on the gentrification of Brooklyn, could there be a duller subject? I yawned. Famously, my breath causes the desert wind, so of course a yawn of such ferocity blew the mason jar right out of your hand and set your beard alight. I felt bad, so I let you come home with me. Predictably, I regret it. Particularly at this moment as you're propped up on one scrawny arm explaining ISIS to me, of all people.

3. I am Manasa. I am pretty much the last goddess you should have told to 'smile' on the subway. Nothing angers me more than being told to cheer up. Actually, there is one thing that infuriates me even more and that is when humans refuse to worship me! Man, I hate that. I've had it bad enough all my life with my dad and my husband (ex-husband) being a couple of bozos. On top of that, my stepmother was super mean to me. Who do you think burnt out one of my eyes!? No bloody wonder I'm grumpy and sad. Then along you came with that goofy grin, doling out the orders disguised as cheer. No,

I will not smile. The reason you are lying here beside me is sheer bloody-mindedness on my part. I descended to earth to obtain human devotees and last night on the 4 train you made yourself known. I like a challenge: you may mock me at first, but I will rain calamity down upon you until you treat me right. It's monsoon season back home and we have a long day ahead of us, buster. So, off you go. Double shot flat white with a splash of half and half, and two sweet 'n' lows. I'll wait right here, be careful not to let the cobras out.

4. I am Athena. I guess you're wondering why I invited you back to my place last night when I had no intention of having sex with you. For one thing, we just met! I'm not like that. I know, I know, it's New York City. Believe me, I know. I'm actually the Goddess of the City *and* the protectress of civilised life. Speaking of which, I enjoyed your cello playing. You seem clever and thoughtful and you promised me you were checked out last year and came up clean. There really was no need to tell me about the crab case of '98 but I appreciate it. Another reason you are worthy of my esteem is that you work in finance *just so you can earn the optimum amount of money to donate to charity*. You're an altruist – hurray! That's why I rescued you from that boring party and brought you back here with me. I'm not denying that we have mega-chemistry, OK? But I am warning you, I'm a virgin for

life. Once a friend of mine saw me naked and I was so furious I put his eyes out. What am I like? We laugh about it now but at the time he was pretty upset. So – shall we just snuggle?

5. I am Medb. Old Irish spelling: mɛðv; Middle Irish: Medb, Meadb; Early Modern Irish: Meadhbh, mɛɣv; Modern Irish: Méabh, mʲeːv, Medbh or Maebh; sometimes Anglicised: Maeve, Maev or Maive. I was totally floored when you wrote all of those variations on my Shake Shack burger order docket. Usually in this town, nobody has even heard my name before. As soon as my buzzer lit up and I studied my docket, I knew I had to meet you. Then, I thought I should probably finish my Shake Shack burger and crinkle fries and peanut butter milkshake first. So I did. Then, burping slightly, I made my way up to the counter and introduced myself. The rest, as they say, is history. Or mythology, whichever. Who cares? All I care about are the following three things. Are you without fear, jealousy or meanness? Yes? Then let's do this.

Subletting Straight
to My Heart

Borrowing a stranger's life is not a new idea – conmen and shysters have been doing it forever. They steal a passport and a credit card belonging to poor old Marjorie Magee then fly to Panama in their brand new pair of Air Jordan 2s and continue to swindle their way around town until Marjorie figures out that she didn't simply misplace her identity – it was robbed! I can't say I blame those chancers. Being limited to one life and one identity when there are so many possible existences to be had makes me sad. Particularly when so many decisions are made for us, like our eye colour and our IQ. In my case that's murky blue and almost 17, but I'm working on the latter by doing jigsaws and trying to focus on complex TV shows like *Scandal*. Where we are born and when, and what race and gender we are, the traits and tricks that lie in our DNA – all of these are written. Other decisions, if we are lucky, we get to make ourselves: how to dress, what to work as, where to live. The first two are easy – wear something tight and do something helpful. That last one though, where to live? It pains my goddamn heart.

One summer, I spent a few days in Paris where people drink bowls of warm milk and purr at each other in cafes. They are cats, you see. Stylish, well-fed cats with the ability not only to speak, but to speak French. I stayed in a pretty little apartment on the Rue du Regrette and, true to its name, the place made me rue and regret. I rued the day I chose to go to college in Coolock instead of Montmartre. I regretted the time spent trawling through Oprah Winfrey's Instagram instead of learning the French for 'one more slice'. *This world is so big*, I thought, as I looked at a brand new place I would never have enough time to get to know, *and I'm just a bozo living on my knees*.

As I wandered around the cobbled streets of the Cathedral district, refusing to acknowledge people begging for change, these big questions plagued me – what sort of life should I lead? Who should I be? How can I test out the best ways of living? I tried to distract myself by visiting Notre Dame and playing the age-old game of 'which gargoyle I'd sleep with if I had to sleep with one'. I chose a little hunched figure of indeterminate gender crouching over the west entrance. It had a stony little face, as you'd expect, but an athletic torso and great shoulders. I stared up at my sexy little monster and tried to figure out how I'd explain our union to my family. As is so often the case, as soon as my brain began struggling over a new problem, a solution for the previous problem, of who I should be, popped into view.

I high-fived my little gargoyle and ran off. I didn't look back. I couldn't bear to see the mute mourning in the creature's hollowed-out eyes as it watched me go. And what was my big idea? Subletting! I could borrow other homes and thereby other lives; I could try them on for size and figure out what suited me in a completely acceptable and non-shyster way – I could sublet.

The first nest I cuckooed my way into belonged to a pair of scientists in North London They were leaving to do some research in New Zealand and I sublet their apartment for three months house when I first moved to England. I was excited to start my new life as a Londoner in a house full of handmade quilts made by someone else's mother; I downplayed the scary parts of the neighbourhood. Turnpike Lane is on the Piccadilly Line, I told myself brightly, which leads directly back to Heathrow Airport!

Between the Tube station and my new home was a laneway with no name, until my instincts gave it one. 'Stab Alley' is an L-shaped path running between a huge shopping centre and a street of terraced houses with little front gardens piled high with stained mattresses and broken toys. Because of its shape, it's not possible to see the alley through from end to end, making it approximately 40 times more frightening than a regular alley. However, when the council were threading barbed wire across the metal spikes on top of the graffiti-proof concrete walls, they thoughtfully erected large circular mirrors on either end. So when you turned the alley corner, you could see what lies ahead. In all likelihood it would be too late to run from whatever lurked there, but you could at least see who or what was about to kill you. I looked in those mirrors every day, fully expecting to see a strangling enthusiast or a rabid badger, but only ever seeing my pinched, white face hurrying by.

There was another mirror that loomed large in my life there. It was on the wall of the scientists' bedroom, covered with swirly text saying things like 'Absolutely stunning – you are beautiful – look at your nose – it's unrepeatable – woah woah woah – you are a wonder.' The words obscured my reflection, making it impossible to put my make-up on, so I never used that mirror. I covered it with a black scarf as is traditional in my culture. Here is what I gleaned from the house's occupants – they were married to each other, enjoyed hiking and had a case of wine delivered each month. They had an expensive bread-maker and the most frustrating collection of lidless Tupperware I've encountered to date.

I heard a terrifying story once about a woman who filled

her bathroom cabinet with marbles so she would know when her dinner party guests were nosey-parkers. They'd snoop their way into her cabinets and the marbles would cascade out, crashing onto the ground, alerting everyone to their poking preoccupation. In a sublet there are no such dangers. The whole point is that the person is not home.

It's rude, of course, to go through someone else's things, but I find that by simply pretending I'm looking for Super Glu, any qualms can easily be expunged. Sometimes I truly do need Super Glu, having broken something that doesn't belong to me, like a picture frame holding a photo of someone's Native American great-grandmother, or someone's great-grandmother dressed up as a Native American for a fun costume party.

I cannot explain my compulsion to poke around and gather information. I don't have an end in mind. I've come across all sorts of things in various sublets including extremely esoteric porn (2006 cat calendar with Pope Benedict's head pasted on Miss February's reclining body), evidence of insurance fraud (a fake shoulder-to-wrist cast) and secret stashes of semi-sweet chocolate drops (this one is true and I've got the blood sugar levels to prove it). I am an entirely objective observer when I live in someone else's home. I'm not like, 'What's this? Extra-wide tampons – wahey, that poor bitch.' I'm just a witness, man, not a judge. In fact, apart from you, I don't even tell anyone about what I find.

That was my defence when I lived with my sister and she'd go into a rage over my nosiness. She'd say to me, coldly, 'Maeve, why did you move my running magazines and stack up the coins on my dresser?' I'd tell her I was just looking around, for no reason. Once I added weakly, 'I'm a writer and as such am full of curiosity,' and she said, 'You're a fucking weirdo, more like.' I thought to myself, *I'm sure I can be both a writer and a weirdo, I mean, look at Hemingway*, but I knew better than to say that out loud. My sister hates Hemingway!

I sublet in New York too, when I first got here. I found a place on Craigslist. For those of you reading this in the future, which is all of you, Craigslist was, and possibly still is, a website, and will always be an easy lay. You put down the money and Craigslist will give you what you're after, no questions asked. I got just what I wanted – a studio on Bergen Street in Park Slope for a month. It belonged to a cello player who was going on tour with a bluegrass band. He was curly haired and mightily shy. I got the feeling he wished his cello would pop him in the case so he could be the one wheeled around silently until it came time to play. I loved my time reading his copy of *Gulliver's Travels* sitting on his window seat looking down at the summery street three storeys below. We spoke briefly as I handed back the keys and I watched as he turned bright red when I told him the sheets were in the launderette. Maybe it's because

I added, 'I mean, nothing *happened* to them, I just thought it was good manners to wash them.' 'Sure, that's cool,' he mumbled, mortified. I shrugged and got a cab to my new apartment. A home at last – a somewhat permanent nest for this little pelican after months of moving around!

I was secretly very proud of not having a home for two years. Before I left Dublin I gave away all my furniture and reduced everything I owned down to two suitcases. I also left a giant desk and four paintings in my parents' house, but I left those items out of the stories I told about how nomadic and free I was. In conversation with new people, I would often manage to mention my vagabond existence. 'Oh it's pretty easy for me to move around because I just have two bags.' Then I'd do an apologetic smile and they would rush to reassure me that this was nothing to be embarrassed about. They would often say they wished they could be so minimalistic and unmaterialistic. I would sort of wince and say that stuff never really mattered to me. When I felt that things were going really well, I'd add that Mahatma Gandhi owned just one pair of sandals and two robes when he died. In that way, I modestly placed myself as one down from Gandhi in the scale of goodness.

I kept this up until my mother referred to my paintings when I was home at Christmas. 'You know, this house isn't a hotel.' An abstract reference for her to choose but they were, after all, abstract paintings. Of course, saying the house wasn't a hotel didn't exactly make sense. She should have said, 'this isn't an art gallery,' or, 'this isn't a storage facility,' but she said hotel. As sure as she is my mother and my eyes resemble hers more and more with every passing minute – I knew what she meant. She meant that I shouldn't leave my paintings there any longer. She meant I was acting like a dickhead. She was right.

Things have weight. Objects mean something. Places hold feelings. One afternoon, sitting in my borrowed bedroom in North London, I started thinking about this old glazed plant pot I used to have in my house in Dublin. It was mustard-coloured and a bit too big for the fern it held. It was pleasantly round and cool to the touch. There was a crack up one side of it, not a bad one. It was sturdy and functional and always on the sill, holding the fern with its light green leaves spilling forth prettily.

Now, though, I couldn't remember where it was. One of my friends had taken it, maybe. Before we moved out, we had this two-day festival where we put everything into a huge pile in the middle of the room. We invited everyone over to take their pick. People seemed sad about it, but I forced jollity onto the occasion. I genuinely felt giddy at the time. This was liberating! Who needs stuff? Take it! Now, I emailed everyone. *I know this is silly, please disregard if not – but have you got my plant pot? That mustard-coloured one with a crack in it?*

When I got to my new apartment in Brooklyn, not a sublet – an actual rental – my friend showed me around and said, 'You know how, in every New York apartment, there's a thing?'

'A thing? Like, a cat?' I asked hopefully.

'Nah,' he replied. 'A thing like either a really cool secret thing or a really terrible secret thing.'

I didn't know that, but I nodded in a calm way like I do when someone says a sex act I've never heard of and plan to look up later. It turned out that in my new apartment, there really was a terrible secret thing. The shower was in a tiny, homemade room in the kitchen, just next to the oven.

From the outside, it looked like a broom closet. From the inside, it felt like a murder box. There were two feet of floor space to undress on before stepping up a steep incline to a salmon-coloured shower tray. The tray and mismatched shower doors were home to lush patches of mould, absolutely flourishing in its dream environment. There was no ventilation. A flickering fluorescent light dangling from exposed wires illuminated the nightmare perfectly. It was the perfect shower to cry in.

Sometimes I would worry about the lack of ventilation and leave the door open a crack, but that was impractical at mealtimes – the smell of frying onions would sink into my skin. A shower view was not ideal for my housemates either. I mean, have you ever tried eating when you're super turned on? There was only one aspect of the tiny airless murder room that I appreciated – there was no space for a mirror. Most bathrooms have at least one mirror and I always find them distracting. I stand naked in front of them, puffing out my stomach to see what I'd look like if I were pregnant. I complement this look with a benevolent smile – the calm one pregnant women have. Then I try sucking in my stomach so my ribs show to see what I'd look like if I were anorexic. The face I make to match that look is 'sad but determined'. Then I try to do both to see if that's possible. Before I know it, half an hour has gone by and I have to leave the house with wet hair again.

In December, our landlord told us he was going to put in a new bathroom. I didn't take much notice because he said the same thing about putting in a new kitchen and that took almost ten months to complete. The project became as slow-moving and impossible to criticise as a Beckett play. The landlord would appear in the kitchen, beer in hand, and dreamily attach a new handle to the cutlery drawer. He would leave only to return weeks later, beer still in hand, to gaze at the spice rack thoughtfully, before disappearing again.

Like frogs in gradually boiling water, we grew sleepy and forgot our DIY skills. We got used to opening the press with a spatula and balancing the juicer on the hob. The seasons changed three times as we stepped over the half-finished tiling. I expected no less of a drawn-out job on the bathroom either, but something came over the landlord that winter. A kind of fog lifted, he had some kind of spiritual awakening that led to a letter saying he needed us to leave the apartment for the month of January. He was going to put in a new bathroom and increase the rent. I couldn't help feeling proud of him. He was behaving like a real landlord! Then I felt worried for myself. Leaving aside the rent hike, I had to find somewhere to live for a month. I heard faint keening from across the Web and I knew that before long, I'd be back on my knees once more, in front of that reliable old whore – Craigslist.

That seductive idea came rushing back: once again I could choose my own adventure, be a new person in a new house, try out another life. This time I would be a yoga teacher in Park Slope, with a dog. I flapped across the park as she spread her wings in India. I never met her, simply picked up the keys and the leash from the locker downstairs. There were clues to her personality everywhere, as you'd expect in someone's home. Now, lest you think I'm jumping to conclusions, I am aware that clues can send you in the wrong direction. For example, one of my aforementioned paintings is of foxgloves. You may reasonably deduce from that that I like flowers and/or purple. Fine. However, the real reason I own that painting is that the idea of foxes wearing poisonous petals as gloves has thrilled me since childhood

So – far be it for me to decide on what this lady's aesthetic choices say about her. It was just very difficult not to, because her décor was so literal. The clues were actually spelled out on the walls. There were words everywhere. It said 'Believe' in swirly silver writing over the bedroom door and written on smooth rocks on the bedside table were the words 'Live' and 'Laugh'. There was a smooth bronze disc beside the toilet painted with the word 'Empathy'.

What kind of person needs to think of empathy while using the toilet? Why did she need to be reminded to laugh by a pebble? What was it that she had to believe? I wondered if she had a brain injury. The day after I got there I plugged the heater into the wall and the power went out in the room. I couldn't talk to the building's super because subletting wasn't strictly allowed, so for three days we emailed back and forth. Between crystal healing and reiki classes, she managed to type, 'I lived there for 10 years and this never happened!! Do NOT call an electrician that will be TOO expensive.' Her cyber-yelling was followed by her automatic sign off, *In love and service,* which was followed by her made-up Sanskrit name.

These days, the sheen of subletting has worn thin. I don't want to do it anymore. My plan didn't work. Despite living in these people's homes, sleeping in their beds, using their possessions – I didn't know what it was like to actually be them. I hadn't earned a PhD in geophysics or learned how to play the cello or mastered a solid crow pose and fallen in love with a girl. And as for their things, the possessions they owned? They were just clues. No matter how hard I looked in from the outside, I could never really know what it was like to be another person. I would always be me, trying on other lives but unable to get comfortable, gradually realising that none of them would ever fit and that all I could do was make one of my own.

Notorious
Shoe Returner

Whenever I smell cardamom I think about how men are stronger than women. Physically, and I'm generalising. You know women, we're always generalising. I was subletting a room in an apartment for a month and the man that lived there, Jeff, was friendly and annoying. I was friendly and aloof, and he didn't like that. Whenever he cooked he asked if I wanted to join him for dinner. I always said no, every time. In the beginning I'd give him a reason. Sometimes I'd lie. 'No thanks, I'm dining at Per Se later on and thence to the opera.' Other times I'd tell him the somewhat bleak truth. 'Oh, I'm good – I just inhaled a $6 burrito in my room.' After two weeks of this, he would still ask if I was hungry, just in a more pained way. I would mumble, 'No, but thanks,' and then go into my room and wonder what it was about his persistent offerings that made me so furious.

The nice girl in me chastised the other girl in me. I wasn't even sure which girl that was – the unkind one, the honest one, the one who didn't feel comfortable around Jeff? Whichever one continually rejected his friendship, or maybe his passive-aggression. It was confusing. I knew sharing food was an act of friendship, and I knew I didn't want to be friends.

We shared the kitchen and bathroom, and he could hear when I left my room to use either of them. He would sometimes pop out just as I unlocked the bathroom door to say things like 'Hey – I got a new lamp, I'd like you to come see it. I know you're not interested but I'm just trying to be social here!'

'OK,' I would say, smiling woodenly, making no reference to his comment about me not being interested. Then I would stand and look at his lamp and say things about it. Factual things, things you say to a parent about their new-born baby who has not yet developed any distinguishing features. 'Wow – it sure seems bright.'

Other excruciating encounters happened in the kitchen, like when he came in as I was cooking and said, 'I love that coconut smell, is it your hair?' And I replied, 'Nope – it's the omelette.' And we talked for a few minutes about coconut oil and how I have a boyfriend.

Jeff began to knock on my door to show me his new shoes and ask my opinion on them. My mistake was being too enthusiastic the first time he did it. I think I said something like, 'What a nice brown – perfect for an office setting.'

A couple of days later he was back, with two pairs. He did a mini fashion show as I stood there, bewildered. I didn't care about his shoes. I don't even care about my own shoes. When my left boot split I glued it with Super Glu and jammed it under a coal bucket to stick it back together. As he paced the hall modelling a loafer, Jeff, in a conspiratorial tone more suited to saying something interesting, said 'The thing about me is, I'm notorious for returning shoes.'

He was notorious, for returning shoes. Throughout the land, shoe salesmen whisper his name in awe and fear. At conferences they recount the man, the legend. They tell how Jeff stalks around shoe shops, glancing in those low mirrors, seemingly happy. He pays up, leaves the shop with a box under his arm and that's the end of the story. Until the next day – BRAP BRAP – Jeff's back! The Notorious Shoe Returner is relentless in his returning of all kinds of shoes – brogues, loafers and boots. None of them are quite what he is after – some are a little loose on the heel, he has concerns about the durability of others. This shade of black is not dark enough, apparently, the shape of the toe a little too casual. At his funeral, the eulogy will surely centre on this fascinating personality quirk. The speaker will take a deep breath, steady herself on the lectern, as she says, *The thing about Jeff was, he was never fully satisfied with any one pair of shoes. In fact, he was notorious for returning them.* Cue an enormous wail from the gathered mourners.

The cardamom was the final farewell to any semblance of a couple of friends that chose to live together or indeed any hint of a romantic couple who chose to be together. I was in the kitchen and Jeff came in, asking what I was doing. I told him I was making soup. A classic exchange, vintage stuff, really. He told me I should put some cardamom in it. I had no intention of putting cardamom in it but I agreed. Then he said, 'I don't think you've got any over there – but you can use mine.'

I replied, a little too quickly, 'That's OK, I have some. Thank you though.'

He barked a laugh. 'I'm pretty sure you don't because I didn't see any in the spice rack when I looked last week, that's why I bought some.'

'It's OK, really.' I insisted. 'I have some.' It wasn't true – I didn't have cardamom.

I just wanted Jeff to go away, but of course he wouldn't.

'Are you sure you even know what cardamom is?'

I nodded, unable to say anything because the air was too thick with the peculiar tension of a man who is angry with a woman because she is not doing what he wants her to do.

'Look,' he said. 'I'm going to leave it here and you can use it if you want to.'

He took his goddamn cardamom off the shelf and put it on the counter.

'I definitely don't want it,' I said.

'Alright,' he said. 'Just smell it so you know what it is.'

With a hard smile, he crossed the kitchen and held the cardamom up to my face. I smelled it. I didn't have a choice.

The Judge Make Time

As you know, I am an important and powerful business woman with an absolutely hectic international schedule. It was in that capacity that I was visiting Dublin from New York. It was nothing to do with seeing my endocrinologist for free rather than paying for health insurance in America, oh no. Anyway, I boarded the bus to Dublin airport one fine June morning. Public transport, cheap early morning flights, packing my own lunch – all of this helps me to feel like one of the people. I behave like I'm on the TV show *The Secret Millionaire* where the protagonist pretends to be poor, mixes it up with a bunch of have-nots, then at the end says, 'Gotcha! I'm actually mega-rich! Here's a fiver for your troubles. Byeeee!' Except that I actually don't have money and if I did, I wouldn't give it to a community centre for abandoned donkeys in some awful part of the midlands.

The accumulation of wealth is not one of my ambitions. This doesn't make me a better person than someone who does want to be rich, but it does makes me *feel* like I'm a better person than them. If I became wealthy I am convinced that, like any other human being, I'd turn into a little devil. Instead of getting the bus to the airport, I'd get a giant car and an even bigger driver to drop me off, then plonk myself on a couple of high stools at those odd little seafood bars where I would eat thousands of oysters before paying an old woman to lift me to my gate, kicking her on with my diamanté spurs, all the while shouting into my phone over her groans.

I am not rich, but I did have some money that morning. Enough to kick off the almost unbelievable chain of events that I'm about to relay to you now, if you think you're ready. How do you know you're ready? Are your bowels empty and your pupils fully dilated? Then you're ready, friend. Here we go.

I had in my possession fifty big ones, in one note. Cast your mind back to before the bust, when the Irish People were booming children. Then you may recall the note I mean. That mustard-coloured piece of paper that used to be so common in Ireland before the Celtic Tiger was made into a rug. Anyway, I handed my €50 note to the driver and said, 'Single, please.' That wasn't a question about his relationship status, it was just the type of ticket I needed.

The driver took the note and gawked at it reverently for a while, then buried his head in his hands. Looking up, he said pitifully, 'You'll wipe me out! I'll have no change all day because of you!' He was being melodramatic and I quite enjoy that in a man, so I humoured him by agreeing to get change myself.

My exact words were, 'OK, I'll go and pick up a healthy snack or maybe a herbal tea and come back with change.' I delivered this line as best I could, but because it was not true, it sounded empty. I thought that was why the driver seemed hesitant when he replied, 'Grand. I'm not due to go for another five minutes so you have a bit of time.' I curtsied and hopped off the bus, straight into the station to look for chocolate. 'Seek and ye shall find,' as Curly said to Wurly.

Next thing you know, I'm back beside the driver, cheap chocolate melting in my pocket, change in my hand, ready to give our relationship another go. I presented my brand-new-smaller-than-before notes and sang out, 'Here you go, exact change!'

The driver seemed different, less beaten-down. He was almost confident as he looked right at me and said, 'Grand, I won't be leaving for around 20 minutes, love, so take a seat.' Love!? In the three minutes since we first met, he'd grown fonder of me than I could have hoped. Touching, but hardly surprising. I must have brightened up his day with my helpful attitude and adorable peepers shyly looking out under even more adorable bangs. And yet, 20 minutes? I wondered about the delay. I looked at him closely, and realised with horror that he was a completely different man. It's not that all bus drivers look the same to me, no no I assure you. It's those identical uniforms and identical buses – that's how they get you!

My confusion quickly turned to a cold fury that filled me from head to toe, taking in the whole torso and butt area as it went. Words like 'betrayal', 'you have a bit of time' and 'missed flight' swirled around my mind. The other driver had left without me! Through the windscreen, my eyes spotted this Judas and his Last Supper of a bus. They were stalled at a red light. That's when my body took over. My heart sped up and my legs took immediate action. I leapt from the second bus and absolutely bolted toward the first.

Plyometrically speaking, it was something else. I sprinted across two tram lines and leapt over a little traffic island, clearing foliage as I went. I nipped in front of a car, rapping its bonnet sharply three times to alert the stunned motorist inside that I was in full control of my movements. I skidded up to the door of the bus just as the lights went green.

An urban sophisticate like me knows the rules of the road. I mean, I can't drive so I don't actually know the rules of the road but I know the street rules. I'm streetwise. Well, I'm not streetwise in a way that I know the names of drugs and I can tell who's a narc. Look, what I mean is, I always use public transport and I totally know that you're not allowed to get on a bus unless the bus is at a bus stop. However, on this day, at this time? The rulebook was out the window.

My breath fogged the glass door of the bus as I came to a halt. With a swipe of my sleeve I made a little window in the condensation and peered through it, shaking my head and tapping the glass lightly with my forefinger. The driver swivelled in his seat like the serpent he was, his eyes widened ... I was back, and madder than ever. Shocked to his core, his hand shook as he pressed the door button. I clambered aboard.

'Well, well, well,' I said – calm, focused.

'I ... I ... was looking for you,' he stuttered.

I shot back, secretly trying catch my breath, 'Well, you clearly didn't check the bridal magazine section of the newsagents.'

His muttered defence? 'I couldn't leave the bus.'

'Ha!' I said. 'The bus is a big boy.'

Looking back, my saying that didn't fully make sense. The driver probably didn't mean that the bus gets nervous when it's alone. It was more than likely an insurance thing, but that doesn't even matter because I said, 'The bus is a big boy' with such cool menace. I followed it up with the absolute zinger. 'Here's your money ... no change required.' I was tempted to tuck the change into his blazer pocket to make him feel cheap, but he was cowering so much I couldn't reach. Instead I simply pressed the money into his hand, folded his fingers over it and left it at that.

I settled into my seat, directly behind the mirror, so I could glare at The Sneak whenever he raised his eyes from the road. He didn't dare, so I sat back and relived my triumph. The intelligence and quick thinking I'd shown in figuring out what to do, the courage to run straight into traffic, the sheer physical prowess I'd demonstrated. The magnificence of me altogether! I wished that there had been more witnesses than just that stunned motorist in the Yaris. There was only one other passenger on the bus, and he didn't seem interested in congratulating me, despite my looking at him a number of times and doing a 'Can you believe me?' face at him.

It's a sad truth of my life that many of my victorious moments go unnoticed by others. I thought about that as I sat in the airport eating my cheese sandwich, almost three hours early for my flight.

The thing is, I hate being late. When you're late, everybody can see that you are a disorganised mess, unable to deal with adult life. And that's exactly the kind of thing I need to keep secret! Being late is my nightmare, my scariest nightmare. Scarier even than getting into bed and touching my bare foot onto a living carp or pike and that carp or pike stirring sleepily. I can't even bear being late for things I don't want to do. Dental appointments, hen nights, funerals – I'm there with ten minutes to spare. It's not easy. Not as easy as sending a series of *'There in 5 … sowwy'* text messages and definitely not as easy as arriving whenever you feel like it.

It wasn't always this way. If you were an investigative journalist with an 'in' to Walterstown National School, you could find evidence in writing of my consistent tardiness. Before I explain myself, I should explain the system I was operating within. In Ireland, national school means primary school, elementary school. In Walterstown National School, you start off as a four-year-old in Junior Infants, then move on to Senior Infants.

I love the idea of being a *Senior* Infant, imbued with all the wisdom and business acumen an infant could carry. *I beg your pardon, Madame, I am a SENIOR infant and as such I do NOT need you to explain sub-prime mortgages so please can you just finish peeling my mandarin orange for me in silence?*

In some rural schools, Junior Infants are called 'Baby Infants', in case there is any doubt about just how young they are. They can get away with anything. *You must understand that I'm simply a baby infant. How was I to know this was your parking spot?* In my friend's school in Kildare the youngest children were in 'Low Babies' and moved to 'High Babies' in their second year. I suppose that, over the summer, they just chilled, smoking trees errday.

Walterstown National School is a big old redbrick

rectangle with wooden windows and a little porch at the front. It's a ten-minute walk from my family home. My father and his brothers and sisters and my grandfather and his brothers and sisters had gone to school there too, though not at the same time as us. When I attended, it was a two-room school holding around 70 children and two teachers.

As well as learning to read and write, we did all the usual activities associated with a 1980s childhood in Ireland, like spinning three times in the teacher's chair when it was our birthday and whispering our sins to male virgins clad in black so they could tell us which prayer to use in begging the Lord's forgiveness.

Unusually for the time, the school had Meeting Book, an A4 hardcover notebook left under the chalkboard for us children to write our concerns in. These concerns were discussed at the weekly meeting, held on a Friday before the spelling test. They always began with, 'I would like to bring up about', and included worries about people being mean to each other or the mystery of the sticky tape that had gone missing from the art cupboard.

It was during one of these meetings that I realised with a sharp flash of devastation that:

1. my family were flawed
2. that flaw was noted by others, and
3. that flaw affected others.

The Meeting Book entry read: *I would like to bring up about one particular set of Higginses who are always late for school and I can't concentrate when they come in and rustle around in their coats and whisper.*

That's what it said. Now – the collective noun for Higgins is not 'a set' – it's a Huddle – but the meaning was clear. There were three Higgins Huddles in the school. There were my siblings and I, then there were our cousins whose father, my uncle, is almost identical to my father except he is taller and has a higher voice, which may be something to do with his height. These days, my father and my uncle's grandchildren sometimes mix the two of them up. All they see are smiling white moustaches and tired eyes. I love nothing more than attending a first birthday party where the confused baby gets passed from one to the other saying balefully, 'Gandad? Nooooo. Gandad?' and we all laugh, my uncle's girlish giggle giving him away. There was also a third, unrelated Higgins Huddle in our school made up of two sisters with fair hair who for some reason played the bagpipes.

My sisters and brother and I were the original Higginses – dark-eyed, pink-cheeked, good at spelling and late for school. That was our signature move – we were always late for school. I was aware of it, but didn't realise anyone else was. School started at the somewhat arbitrary time of 9.10am and we would wander up the road and get there for about 9.20, maybe 9.30 if the baby was acting up or someone dropped a glove or saw a dead badger.

It turned out that, despite our whispering and tiptoes, everyone had spotted us five Higginses coming in late every day. There followed a long discussion about how it feels to be on time for class every morning only to be disrupted by the same people, namely us, day after day. We were treating their time and therefore their lives as less important than our own. The conclusion, drawn by the group, was that we needed to make an effort to be on time. I glowered around the room as my friends and enemies alike said how unfair our consistent lateness was. I felt the helpless anger of the one in the wrong. From that day, I vowed, I would not only be on time for school – I would be early.

As any cuckold with a wanderer on their hands or any dieter with Nutella on theirs will tell you – vows don't always hold. It's not that I didn't make an effort to be on time, I did. In the weeks after our public shaming I would yank the hairbrush out of my sister's hair before she'd completed her second plait and yell at my brother to forget about his long division sum copy, he had to leave it behind – there was no time! We had to rush! Absolutely no blackberry picking on the way, we had to get to school for 9.05am. It worked – we found out for the first time that it was possible to be at our desks in time for roll call. Gradually though, we dawdled our way back into old habits and became the Late Higginses once more, much to my mortification.

This stuck with me, as mortification often does. It hardened, too, into a solid truth I can't help believing to this day, which is as follows – to be on time is to be grown up and responsible and to be late is to waste other people's lives. Aren't I a carefree gal, a whole lot of fun?

The intensity with which I regard time strengthened as I got older and became aware of its finite nature. One autumn evening after school, I watched from our gate as my uncle slowly herded his cattle down the road from the field into their shed for the night. As they plodded past, a parade of eyelashes and swinging black and white, it hit me, and I felt a small sadness plant itself in my heart.

Time is it. It's all we have. We do not know the number of days left, but we know there is a number. The ache I felt that evening returns now as I sit on a bench in Union Square and watch waitresses put chairs on tables and wash the coffee shop floor. Lights flicker on around the city, people nod off on the trains. The day is done. We've raced for buses, left blackberries to rot, ignored our alarms, forgotten to write emails and remembered to send apologies.

Junior Infants become Senior Infants before our eyes and we still don't believe it. We dip and weave and convince ourselves that we have saved time here or spent too much time there, always feeling there is never enough time, and for what? It doesn't matter. The light has faded and you've taken your chances or you haven't. Either way, the dark seals the ending.

One of the things I love about New York City is the daily battle against this inevitable finality. This place is at its most charming when it refuses to obey the laws of nature. At any time of night you can dance, eat, wash your car, go to the gym or drink coffee. *Don't worry, we'll light it up!* says Manhattan. *Look, honestly – it's not over – we're the city that never sleeps!* I want the same thing, my darling city, truly I do, but it's not possible. For all your money and cleverness, you cannot fool the clock. All the electricity in the world, all the 24-hour joints and glittery fun to be had are valiant attempts at immortality, but they reveal a glint of desperation.

I gladly join in this fiction, this hope that we can make time last longer. Of course I do, but that ache remains. Time passes as it must and we can't slow it down, but we can always pretend. That's the least we can do, distract ourselves from its passing a little while longer. So we do, or we try to, until we can't anymore, and then we sleep.

America Runs
on Dunkin'

I love nothing more than the feeling of, in Chelsea Peretti's words 'coffee crankin' through my sys'. I feel powerful, focused, then on edge. Actually, now that my jittery brain comes to think of it, there is one thing I love more than that. I love the smug feeling I get when I am not drinking coffee. When I am, as I tell anyone who will listen, *off caffeine*. I look around at the subway carriage full of New Yorkers sucking on their milky mistress and I feel powerful, in control. I think, *Look at these goddamn sheeple, I used to be just like them, but not today. Today I rely on my nerve and my verve to get me through the day – no stimulants needed!*

O when the mighty fall, we fall hard. This winter, I was back on the coffee wagon, and riding her hard. Every four hours my body would start calling for its medicine, and Mother would have to provide.

In the fancy parts of Brooklyn, it's not difficult to find a place to buy coffee. What's difficult is finding a place that *simply* sells coffee. You're far more likely to come across a bicycle repair shop with a specialty line of flat whites made with house-roasted Incan beans that you have to murmur a special Australian code word for. *Cookaburra*, you whisper, *Julia Gillard*.

It's too much to bear, so to avoid those end-of-the-world, last-gasp days of capitalism scenarios, I began to frequent Dunkin' Donuts. I like their pink and orange colour scheme. I adore their chunky font and I appreciate the insanity of their accessibility – there are two Dunkin' Donuts within walking distance of my house that are open 24 hours a day. Luckily for my life expectancy I don't like their doughnuts, but I've built up quite the collection of unrecyclable polystyrene cups bearing the bittersweet slogan 'America Runs on Dunkin'.' I will refrain from one of those *I like my coffee like my men* gags, although I can confirm that I am irresistibly drawn to powerful men who give me heart palpitations for less than $3.

One evening on my to a show to tell my little jokes and stories, the caffeine demon woke up and began tormenting me. Her main message was that I needed coffee, or I would be a terrible comedian that night and forevermore. I know better than to argue with any of my shrieking demons – they speak the truth. However, this time it was tricky to obey – I was in the illustrious Park Slope, home of $5 million homes, far from my old pal Dunkin'. I looked around desperately until I spied through a window decorated with miniature hay bales and covered in old-timey writing a Gaggia machine.

I steeled myself and entered. As the cowbell tied to the door jangled news of my arrival, I stepped inside, sniffed the air and promptly froze. I was a soldier who'd fought bravely on the breakfast battlefield a long time ago, I thought I'd gone on with my life, I thought I'd put this all behind me … but one sniff and I was pulled back to the torment once more, reminded of my anguish by that unmistakable, hellish stench – porridge.

'What is this place?' I stammered a little, unusual for me, but PTSD (porridge traumatic stress disorder) does that.

'We're a pop-up artisanal oatmeal house.'

The answer to my question came from a bored-looking 18-year-old with the side of her head shaved. I can never tell if that particular look is an indication of electric shock therapy or a powerful aesthetic statement that tells the world, *That's right, one side of my head may look like the torso of a recently neutered cat but I want you to know I did this on purpose and I still look great.*

I suppose it would be rude to ask; in any case, I had just

one more question for the sole employee of this little shop of porridge-horror.

'But. But – why?' I asked. Small word – big question, a question I've been asking since I was old enough to talk. 'Why porridge?' is a question I first directed toward my father, David Higgins, the chief porridge proponent, the oatmeal dictator, the Pol Porridge Pot. Every weekday morning, without fail, we ate porridge for breakfast.

If you're looking for proof of the sheer stupidity of children, listen to this. My brother and sisters and I believed that breakfast cereal was a weekend treat. What a bunch of tiny idiots; our father told us so and we bought it. Sometimes, even outside of therapy, I talk about that lie we were fed. Literally fed! I never regret sharing the truth of my past. Sometimes, other people are cracked open inside by my generosity when they tell me their parents' crazy lies about what constitutes a treat. Stories of grapes and baby carrots being lorded over them as delicacies have shaken me up, sure, but also helped me to forgive my own parents.

I dreamt of unfettered access to breakfast cereal, which has, of course, its own dark legacy. Puffs, shreds and crunches are nothing but textures and noises, I'm sure they are not substantial enough to constitute a meal. There was once a whole marketing campaign based on the idea that a specific bowl of cereal could be a meal by itself but the brand ceased production after teenage girls used the empty boxes to form Ouija bowls to eat this peculiarly demeaning cereal from. If you did this twice a day for a week, Satan himself would show up in the form of self-loathing, easy to spot in his little red swimsuit. You'd lose weight temporarily but the demon would stick around for good.

Anyway, I came up in the 1990s when British 'lads' magazines gained popularity. I didn't read them then, but I remember gazing longingly at a carefully staged photograph of an editorial meeting in one of their super-rebellious offices. You know the offices, divided into cubicles full of ashen-faced, inexplicably smug 30-year-old Englishmen? My eyes were drawn to bowls half full of leftover milk and soggy Sugar Puffs in the background. Cereal for dinner? Cereal whenever you felt like it? The massive sense of sociopathic control you must feel when you manipulate images of naked women all day? That's the kind of life I wanted – very cool.

These man-children editing topless photos of women and writing longingly about cars had the same idea as the Higgins children: unfettered access to sugary cereals represented pure autonomy, complete freedom to make poor choices, the most you could hope for in life. As an 11-year-old girl, I yearned for a job at *Nuts*.

'Why?'

The girl with half a head of hair repeated my question as

she took me in with a cursory glance, then she answered it, 'Cos from November to April we're doing this oatmeal thing. The rest of the year we sell gelato.'

I felt exposed, vulnerable, at sea.

'What?' I asked, buying time.

'GELATO,' she said loudly, adding, 'That means ice-cream.'

No it doesn't, I thought. *Gelato is different to ice-cream, it's got a higher or lower fat or cream content or something.*

Even through the fog of war, my pedantic streak, however ill-informed, remained intact. That same streak urged me to quiz the girl on why breakfast would be served throughout the day and well into the evening; it was 8pm now, for crying out loud. But I didn't dare. Instead I said, 'Can I just have coffee, please?'

She looked annoyed. 'Sure – I mean, I'll have to make it.'

I nodded mutely, unsure of how else the transaction could proceed.

She switched on the coffee machine and asked if I took sugar.

'No thank you.'

I closed my eyes and concentrated hard on not saying, *I'm sweet enough.*

I was already losing this girl. Cutesy ready-made affectations would surely sound my death knell.

'I do take milk,' I added. She seemed more annoyed than before.

'OK, we've got almond milk.'

She bent down reluctantly and opened a refrigerator door.

'Or yogurt.'

Teenagers love sarcasm, I thought, *this is my way in!*

'Great – I'll have a little of both, just curdle them in.'

She shrugged and picked up a spoon.

'I was joking!' I called out, panicked. 'I'll just take it black.'

She looked genuinely pained as she straightened up and handed me the coffee. I knew by glancing at it that it would taste terrible. I tipped her $2, roughly 75%. *That'll teach her*, I thought.

'Do you want porridge in the morning, love? I'm just going to soak it.' It is night time and my father is standing in the kitchen doorway, smaller now, his hair white. He collected me from the airport earlier today. I'm grown up, or some version of it, sitting at the table and frowning at my laptop because I can't get online. He looks at me hopefully with his tired old eyes, scratching his arm under his dressing gown sleeve. 'OK, Pops,' I tell him softly. 'I'd love that – I'd love to have porridge in the morning.'

He's delighted as he takes out the pot and the oats and measures the water, enough for at least eight people.

Perhaps he's thinking back to simpler times, when he had eight little round-faced children, happy to eat what they were given. He smiles to himself as he soaks the porridge. 'GOTCHA!' I yell, making him jump and drop the wooden spoon with a clatter in the quiet kitchen. The budgies wake up and begin to squawk as I tell him, 'No way am I having porridge, not a hope, can we please get some Sugar Puffs or something? Yock. Turn on the fan! I hate that smell.'

And so it is and so it will always be, world without end. Amen.

Get the Look

I've been wearing clothes since I was about three years old. Before that my mother would coat me in goose fat to keep me warm and I would dart around the house, slipping off surfaces, smelling like a dream. On my third birthday, she wiped me clean and presented me with a pink leotard and a tutu. I trudged and stomped around in it, for comic effect of course, but also for political reasons. I never wanted to be a ballerina. Back then, my favourite T-shirt was slate grey with a faded Mickey Mouse on the front. When I saw a similar one in Urban Outfitters recently, I bought it despite the ludicrous price and the inherent shame of shopping there. Thus, in a way, I've been wearing the same clothes since I was a toddler, with some concessions made for a woman's body. I call my style 'comedy-casual/sexy-dowdy', and it's not difficult to imitate. Here is my style advice, in these handy tear-out pages.

DENIM

I wear jeans, you know. I DO. You people have this idea of me that's, like, so bougie. You people think I live in an eyrie and wear silk culottes and have lovers of every race, but I must protest. I urge you to believe me when I insist that I'm almost just like you! There are plenty of days when I, like you, am denim-clad and unremarkable, with my head down, just trying to get through this.

I wear a plain jean. My dentist will tell you I'm not averse to embellishment – Lord knows she's had to free my tongue piercing from my crystal tooth inserts enough times. So I say, sure, by all means add a funky eel-skin belt or sew a diamanté gun onto your jeans. In truth, though, all you are doing is borrowing drama from one medium and forcing it onto another, a tacky director adding violins to an already moving scene. Nobody (I'm referring to myself) likes to be manipulated, so if you want to be real, slither that belt off and unpick those Swarovskis.

As I recently demonstrated by wearing a T-shirt saying 'The Man' with an arrow pointing up and 'The Legend' with an arrow pointing down, sometimes it's a really great move to let your clothes do the talking. There are plenty of pairs of jeans available with words scrawled across the back pockets – containing secret messages about the wearer's personality, often words like 'sweet' or 'cheeky'. The recent swing toward more lofty ideals is to be welcomed; one elderly man won my respect recently simply by having the word 'judicious' emblazoned on his butt.

As you may know, I happen to live in America now, so I am something of a clairvoyant when it comes to trends about to hit the rest of the world. Here are the main pointers. In the Ireland of the very near future, we will all own guns and everything will soon be available in pumpkin flavour only. Here is some hot sartorial gossip right off the trouser presses. Apparently, Mom Jeans cheated on Dad Jeans … with Boyfriend Jeans. I know! The resulting Baby Jeans are relaxed fit and high-waisted, without a trace of the light blue Dad gene.

And these Baby Jeans, it turns out, are the ideal jeans. Babies, stop rolling around the ground wondering who owns those hands attached to your arms. Focus, please. Sit up straight and hear me now – you cram those chubby legs of yours into that soft, elasticated denim and enjoy this special time, when your dimensions across are exactly the same as lengthways and everyone loves you for it, because the opportunity won't come back around until you're 90.

WINTER COAT
The first thing you'll notice when you elegantly heave on the winter coat I designed is the warm feeling that spreads nicely around the small of your back. That heat is coming from a heat pad I've sewn into the lining. I got it in the chemist. It

feels like a warm, steady hand, don't you think? See? You're not alone at that party anymore! There's someone right behind you, guiding you along. Not in a controlling way, no. More a, 'I'm right here and we can laugh about what this idiot is saying in the car later', sort of way.

A woman once told me that women are good at multi-tasking. Come to think of it, she told me twice simultaneously; verbally and in writing. I believed her because as she said and wrote it she liquidised soup, hired a new COO for her start-up and mended a broken segueway – all the while breast-feeding her baby. I'm assuming it was her baby because she was breastfeeding it. So it follows that us busy creatures need a coat with pockets. Depending on the day ahead, we can fill them with soothers, betting stubs, smartphones or one of those little Tasers you use to zap people you don't agree with.

Listen! In this wonderful coat there are tiny speakers attached to the collar, murmuring encouraging things.

Finally, the colour of the coat is important. Are you a winter or an autumn? A blustery colour somewhere between the two? Just make sure the colour helps your eyes pop, but not in a thyroid problem way. The colours we choose send out a signal to those around us. If you want to look French, wear navy. If you know you'll be working as a spy or you're one of those people who inexplicably pride themselves on being shy, wear taupe. Red says *I'm alive … and I've got needs.* If you want people to know how disappointed you are, choose grey.

My coat is whale-coloured. One morning in Target, I enquired about matching accessories. The girl said they didn't have anything whale-coloured, unless I meant black and white. I explained to her coldly, but with patience, that I did not mean black and white, rather a sort of bluey-charcoal; a colour to flatter my icy skin tone, wavy hair and underwater eyes. She looked at me blankly then, until I put the coat on and did a twirl. The girl came to life, proving that this coat will pull you together and say to barnacles everywhere, *Stick with me kid ... I'll show you the world.*

TIGHTS

Tights are named after the restrictive sensation they cause throughout the leg and pelvic region. Tights are the worst, the original necessary evil. I dread wearing tights more than seeing a rat clambering out of my toilet or hearing an unchecked vegan explaining their motivation. Tights are too close and constantly irritating, they forever need hoiking up and hauling around. Tights make legs look like meat tubes and bodies look like machinated dolls, and not in a good way.

As anyone who's gone to a traffic light disco or driven on a road and used actual traffic lights will know – colours mean something. A woman in brightly coloured tights is transmitting a message, loud and clear. She is clinging to a cliff of despair and pleading: *Help me! I've got a bottomless pit where my personality should be!* Do not help her. Don't you dare extend a hand. Stand back, watch her lose her grip and listen as she tumbles, wailing ... *but I'm quirkkkkyyyyy.* Thud: she's gone. You, get on with your day, remembering always to wear black tights and black tights only. I will only be satisfied when children hiding under tables at all sorts of events, not just funerals, will peep out and see a host of black spidery legs scuttling around busily. I hope you agree with me when I insist upon black tights and black tights only. Well, do you?

Not really, says you, stirring in the bed and rolling over onto one elbow – *what about flesh colour? Surely flesh colour is ideal.*

You're flat on your back, winded now. You have no idea what happened, so I'll tell you. I karate chopped your supporting arm out from under you because I need you to understand my point about flesh-coloured tights. They don't exist. Of course you can buy tights that claim to be flesh-coloured, you can buy anything, but those tights could never mimic what nature has created on this little island of ours. That peachy, bluish hue is all our own, an impossible ideal. OK? Sit up now, have a sip of water.

The wintry truth is this – there is no such thing as a great pair of tights. Tonight, I will open my sock drawer, clear away the sweet wrappers and have a good look at my tights. They will be rolled up in rows like so many sleeping hedgehogs, totally benign. Come morning, all will change. They will yawn and stretch and slowly unfurl into their true selves – treacherous, conjoined serpents. On they will slither, tormenting me until nightfall, when I can shed them with a roar and, no longer frightened, return to my enlightened, untightened, self.

FANCY DRESS PARTIES

When it comes to fancy dress costumes, I'm famed for my quick-fire assessments of who should wear what. As a young child, people would walk by my window and I'd call out helpfully 'ruined princess' or 'definitely a goblin'. It was cute then and it's cute now. Just today I said to my bank teller, 'Eric, with your lurching gait and dead eyes, you're practically a zombie already!' He seemed pleased as he pawed the glass partition.

People say be careful what you pretend to be, for that is what you will become. I don't buy it. I'm not superstitious. I used to be, until I took a faith healer's advice on how to shake it. We were on a boat together at the time, and she told me to stop whistling and to tip a sailor's collar. I did just that and kept my fingers crossed. When the ship's cat looked up at the night sky and sneezed at a shooting star, I knew I was cured of all irrationality (touch wood). I'm not worried that I'll become a witch just because I dress up as one. And I do, often. I wear all black clothes and orange lipstick. Then I take off the pointed hat and people assume I'm an artist and writer, which is what I started pretending to be a long time ago. And that's what I became! Or is it?

Anyway, there you have it – my style advice. I won't throw shade on those of you who decide against taking it. In fact, you may be better off, if slightly more freckled than necessary.

The Biggest and Chattiest Changing Room in the World

This should pigeon-hole me for you alright. They don't suit me at all. In fact, they're perfectly ridiculous. You're quite right someone is playing a joke on me although it's far funnier than you realise.

Charlotte Vale, *Now Voyager*

Wonderful lines uttered by Bette Davis, playing a woman on a cruise ship recovering from a mental breakdown. I know, what a perfect plot! Her character, Charlotte, has shed her usual dowdy dresses and borrowed her glamorous cousin's wardrobe. She looks incredible in the scene – wearing a gorgeous white gown and an evening cape decorated with sparkling beaded butterflies. She meets her date, Jerry, a dream of a man played by Paul Henreid, in the cocktail lounge of the ship. He is knocked out, as he should be. They sit and he sees a little note pinned to her back; it's a reminder from Charlotte's cousin about just how and when to wear the cape. He laughs a little, and says something sweet about how birds can borrow feathers and still be beautiful, but poor old Charlotte spirals into an irretrievable funk and runs off to her cabin.

I went to a ball. I did, you know! And I too was a beautiful bird wearing someone else's feathers, but I didn't care. The ball was held on the Upper West Side, in a fancy hotel of the old school variety. Nothing hip about it, instead they had heavy wool carpets and comfortably worn-down banquet halls, a reliably moneyed aesthetic. The waiters in battered white blazers were so old that they snoozed as they stood and strained to hear our orders. I almost couldn't bear asking one of them for more butter from the kitchen. Far be it for me to be ageist though – so I asked. In fact, the butter he fetched was too hard so I sent him shuffling back again. The ball was a lot of fun; my table was the giddiest, the speeches were outrageous and the petits fours were tragically divine. And me? I felt like a million dollars in a dress I had rented for sixty.

Happy as I was in my golden dress, it was not my first choice in Rent the Runway, a dress rental store in, appropriately enough, the Meatpacking District. From the outside, Rent the Runway looks like an upscale boutique, with designer gowns in the window and elegant employees in black wafting around inside. It's only when you're amongst those gowns, pulling them out and noticing that they are all a little big or slightly too worn or just a tiny bit ... used, that the entire place suddenly feels like a dress-up box at a theatre workshop. I pulled out a few cocktail dresses to try on, mostly black and mostly shaped like the 1950s. I was basically choosing an outfit suitable for my grandson's bar mitzvah. I floundered, until a swan of a girl with blonde hair extensions on her little head and a measuring tape around her slender neck came gliding across the floor to my hapless self, offering assistance.

Ten minutes later I found myself in front of a trio of mirrors spinning around and clapping, actually clapping my hands together, as half a dozen women in various states of undress collectively cooed at how stunning I was. The Swan had zipped me into a strapless fishtail dress, black-and-oyster coloured; a dress that sounds like hell, but looked like heaven. Honestly, I couldn't get over myself. Was I this elegant Grecian statue, animated now through some sartorial spell, with the sole purpose of devastating men and inspiring women? I was light-headed at the prospect of entering the world in this powerful form. Or perhaps I was just dizzy from all the twirling. I floated on up to the cash register to secure my future as Queen of the Ball. Then the magic stopped. The dress cost $320. Not to buy, you understand. To rent for a couple of days, after which my Swan Fairy Godmother would forsake me and I'd turn back into a scullery maid. The rental cost was determined by the retail price and this dress was a Vera Wang number, meaning it cost a lot of money and really got into my head. I'd been Wanged.

I just couldn't do it. I don't mean that I couldn't bring myself to pay that much money for a one-night stand with a dress. I mean, I tried all my credit cards and they were rejected one by one. The women in the line that formed behind me were quiet and respectful throughout the process, unusual in a city of hurry-uppers, but they had seen me in the dress. They understood.

The ordeal ended when a lesser Swan, one of those teenage ones who you can't quite believe will ever become a Swan, led me back to the fitting rooms. There, the light seemed different than before. Harsher somehow, like the faces of the other people in the changing room now that I wasn't wearing my oyster-coloured super-shell. With a heavy heart I settled on a black peplum affair. A mourning dress with a thigh high slit; I would go to the ball as a widow trying to get back in the game. I paid up, and went to leave. On my way out, a glitzy gold party dress caught my eye and cast my mind to casinos and forgotten wedding rings. On first sight, I knew that it was trashy enough to be within my budget. I somehow found the serenity to accept the things I could not change (the cost of the Vera Wang dress), the courage to change the things I could (the black dress for the gold dress) and the wisdom to know the difference.

My first time at Rent the Runway was so perplexing and bittersweet, I never went back to the store. That's right, I stole the gold dress. No, I returned it by mail. I considered renting from them again for a New Year's Eve party, and peeked at their website for inspiration. There is a review section where customers give a short biography at the top, listing their size, shape, height and age as well as other outfits they've rented and how they felt about them. I love these reviews, having spent perhaps three months of my life reading them. The reviews are often accompanied by photos that were taken on the night; sometimes the women crop out their heads which is less fulfilling to look at than full-length, candid shots they've snapped in their bedroom mirrors. My favourites are action shots – seeing the girl at her prom with her date, or on a dance floor screaming along to the track being played. Hanging out on the review pages is like being part of the biggest and chattiest changing room in the world. I spent some time investigating a black sequinned romper from the Robert Rodriguez collection.

A romper is a top and shorts together all in one piece – like a baby would wear, except black and covered in sequins.

I read all the reviews and will now share extracts with you, so you will see how I reached my decision on that particular romper for my particular runway.

Super comfy, fun and easy to wear. Those scratchy sequins though!!!

I wore this romper for night one of my Vegas bachelorette weekend! We went and saw the Britney Spears show and then partied like rock stars in Vegas. Two caveats, one beware of lifting your hands up over your head as the crotch will pull all the way up (but that's what you get when you wear a romper) and two the open circle loopy sequins are super scratchy. I didn't notice it so much after a while but, the next morning all my girls who had been dancing in close proximity to me looked like their arms had been attacked by wild cats. But for the most part it was super awesome!
–Starr

Hey, Starr, this leaves me with some questions. Just how many nights *was* your bachelorette party? Oh, and how was the show? Everyone says it's fantastic; Britney's second act. Also, when you say that raising your arms causes the crotch to 'pull all the way up', just wondering how far is that? I guess we're all different. I hope your girls recover and also that the next time they sustain a dance floor injury they will notice it in time to move away from the wild cat/bride to be.

Rented this outfit for my birthday night! I got compliments the whole night! Great fit & SPARKLES!

A bit tight in the lower region area, LOL, but not uncomfortable.
–AmeliaT-bone

Oh dear. I'm sorry to hear that it was tight down there but glad for you that you can LOL about it.

Queen of the sequins

Wore this for my bachelorette party – pink wig an all! Although you do not feel the sequins scratching you – I woke up the next day and my legs looked like a panther attacked me! I had scratches on my arms, legs and back. It just made for a better story tho – I would rent this romper again even tho I was scratched up because it was totally worth it! The mid section seems to be a bit baggy but that's the way the romper is made and in the end it looks good in pictures so who cares. Great romper!
–SofieMalum

Who cares indeed, Sofie! Also this explains why Starr's bridesmaids didn't remove themselves from her vicinity as she scratched them up all night so thanks for that!

Great romper and worked beautifully with minor addition of shiny black belt

This was a great romper. I wore it for a Saturday Night Fever *party and it worked perfectly. The romper was a bit blocky around the waist so I ended up pairing a shiny black belt with it, which worked great and cinched my waist a bit. Overall I loved the fit and it wasn't tight around the middle (great for women like me who have a small pouch after kids).*
–SandyArt

So the baggy midriff works for some – great to know, thanks! I haven't had kids (that I know of) but I do have a 'small pouch', particularly at certain times of the month. Specifically, times right after I've eaten a 14-inch pizza.

Definitely a unique look and a night I won't forget

Used clothing tape to secure one shoulder and it held all night! Think about how you will use the restroom, since it's a step in outfit. Sequins are scratchy, but that's what chafing cream is for! Pockets were fun and I loved wearing it. Hides all figure flaws so wear it and eat!!
–YolandaKate

Yes! Just what I needed to hear, YolandaKate. You mention in your profile that you're 45. Perhaps those years you have on me have made you more practical. In any case I will absolutely think about how I will use the restroom. I often think about that in advance to be honest. You know, I never heard of chafing cream but I just ordered some online. Grateful for permission to eat – kudos to you girl!

Best dressed!

Worn this for my sister's Bachelorette party with strappy heels and very minimal jewelry. I loved the romper and certainly was best dressed! I only had a few issues: 1) the shorts aren't very long – be cautious if you are larger on the bottom 2) there is no zipper or anyway to get into it without stepping through the neck hole – makes it difficult to get the dress on and off if you have larger hips. These issues were pale in comparison to the compliments I received that night.

–EmilieBar

Come on now, Emilie. It's lousy to upstage your poor sister on her night – I hope you won't do the same on her big day! Actually, I don't know her or your dynamics, so you be you. You mention it's difficult to get the dress on, but you understood you rented and wore a romper, didn't you? Or did you put both legs through one hole? That would explain the difficulty you had getting it on and off. In any case, I now call issues pale all the time and for that I am grateful.

Perfect for Lady Gaga!

I had a lot of fun wearing this. I wouldn't buy it, but it was perfect for a Lady Gaga concert! I could dance around without worrying that any of my lady bits would show. We did wear wigs, so sequins was kind of a bad choice because I got tangled a lot. My only complaint is that the lining kind of rode up in the legs. It did make it look sheer on the legs, which was kind of a cool effect, but I found myself tugging at it a lot.
–AngelaNerdx

I probably wouldn't buy it either, considering the number of vaginas it has been jammed into and tugged out of. In fact, I think I may not even rent it.

Worth it!

I wore this outfit for a night out in Las Vegas. I received so many compliments on the romper. I thought I looked pretty cute for the night. By the end of the night, the sequins had started to rub my skin raw, but I expected that to happen, especially with dancing & walking all night. Even with the cons, I would definitely rent this romper again!
–LaChauncey

Woah, LaChauncey. You expected your skin to be rubbed raw and then it was and you will still rent this romper again? It truly must look great. I'm back on the fence!

This is a great, fun & fashionable outfit to wear for any event, party or get-together!

I have the Wide Hips and the Big Butt, and it is always such a mess trying to find Jeans, skirts, shorts that fit me well, so I was quite worried how this would fit on the bottom ... But, everything fit perfectly, I felt very comfortable in this outfit, and very confident. This is a stretchy type material, so this can fit any body figure you may have! I was receiving compliments left and right from everyone, Women & Men alike!
–MikainLATrick

I absolutely love you, MikainLATrick, whoever you are. I shall now attempt to figure out what my body figure is and if I do decide to rent this romper, I hope to receive compliments from men and women be they straight, lesbian, gay, bisexual, pansexual, transgender, transsexual, queer, questioning, intersex, intergender and or asexual.

Head turner for sure!

I'm pretty tall, so it was a little tight in the lady part area, but as long as it was way off the shoulder, I was good! It's a great outfit for an event where you'll be standing 90% of the time, but it's very uncomfortable to sit in, the sequins don't feel so good on the bottom.
–JackieT

How tall are you? Why didn't you give your height in your bio, Jackie? I think I'm tall, I'm almost 5 foot 8. Will my lady parts be constricted? I can't have that! I just don't know what to think. Perhaps you are over 6 foot. How can you be so stat-oriented in your advice about percentage standing time recommended, yet so vague on that crucial detail?! I'm sorry but part of me is glad the sequins didn't feel so good on your bottom.

I didn't turn heads; I broke necks!

I wore this outfit to the Beyoncé concert in LA at the Staples center. All eyes were on me.
–Jojoxxx

Um … you went to a Beyoncé concert and all eyes were on you?
Come on now.

Fun bachelorette party outfit!

You can't really lift your arms up while wearing this or you'll get a wedgie. Haha. I had to dance with T-rex arms all night! Otherwise, I loved the pockets and the fit around the waist. It was loose up top but the short shorts kept it sexy. It was super fun and flirty. Plus, I could eat whatever I wanted for dinner and still feel sassy in my outfit, while my other friends had to suck in ;) I would not wear this

to a classy event but it was definitely great for a bachelorette party.
–Abi Fendi

Because you didn't put an exclamation mark after 'haha' I fully understood how your night went, Abi. I'm thrilled you still felt sassy because that is important! Nobody on here would assume this romper would be appropriate for a classy event, but I suppose it's good to remind yourself every once in a while!

Love RTR! I've recommended it to all of my friends. My husband actually told his buddy, 'This is the greatest idea for women'

This lady didn't leave her name, or any comments other than the headline above. I love that her husband values a dress rental business over education, contraception, voting rights and even Seamless.

I really loved this Romper. I'm a size 14 and it fit perfectly

I was very concerned about the length of the shorts however I got over it and the night was amazing.
–SamBanLaw

Nice one, Sam, good for you! I am genuinely going to use this as a mantra. 'I got over it and the night was amazing' is what I will repeat to myself over and over again.

Jealous

This little black sequin romper was just right for me. It pushed outside my comfort zone because it was so short so I wore black hose to hide my flaws (aka cellulite) and it worked out great. You can't raise your arms or you will get a wedgie. I love, love, love it and got compliments all night long and sometimes the stink eye from those ladies that were jealous :)
–Megan

Oh Megan, where is your sense of sisterhood? Perhaps the other ladies were just thinking about how great you looked. If it's true that women dress for other women, then you got it wrong. Or right? I'm not sure. I feel so conflicted about this romper!

Wore this to Sleep no More. *Great night and I could be mobile in these little hot pants and heels*

I am usually a 4/6 and this was a 2. It fit JUST right. I have an hourglass body, which I think worked with the cut. The shorts are short, but I did not feel like my butt was falling out.
–JessieMakes

You went to *Sleep no More*? I can't bear that show. The phoney intrigue, the forced sexiness, the weird audience and the religious iconography from my childhood being used as a symbol of freakiness? OK the last one is fair enough, and the props in the show are incredible, but still! Nobody actually *wrote* that show, you know, it's meaningless.

That did it, I decided against the romper. I did, however, go to the party. I wore that old classic, the safe choice, the 'jeans and a top' combination. As I got ready that night, alone in my room, I felt a pang. Where were my sequins? How could I scratch my friends and force them to help me use the toilet now? It was a phantom pain, the pain an amputee feels in a limb no longer there, only worse, because it was never there. Oh dear, I wasn't dressed right. I wouldn't get any stink eye from any ladies. I played it safe, and didn't deserve millions of compliments.

Then I got over it and the night was amazing.

Grey Hair Don't Care

In the spring of 2015, Dascha Polanka dyed her hair grey and that was all I could think about for a week. I saw a photograph of her, standing on a red carpet in a black leather dress with magnificent lilac-grey tresses cascading around her face, like an otherworldly goddess gracing us mortals with one snapshot of pure beauty before she disappeared back into the sea. I knew that I must have her hair.

Despite knowing better, I frequently fix on small cosmetic details and convince myself that until I can achieve them I won't be fulfilled as a person. I quiz my friend Abi on what shade of nail polish she is wearing. What brand is it, how many coats? Somewhere in me I believe that when my nails match hers, my life will match my perception of her life, which in Abi's case is adventurous and glamorous. I feverishly hunt the stacking rings I saw a girl wearing on the subway, so that when I get them I too can be a 19-year-old Korean girl studying UX design at The New School. As I said, these are just details; a change in hair colour is much bigger than a detail. It's a commitment, a statement, a distraction. My career in America was picking up, I was busy again and things were exciting, which is a synonym for scary. This was the ideal time to find a distraction, and my attempts to go grey proved to be just that! Let me break it down for you like this.

Upon seeing the Dascha Polanka photograph, the thought that followed 'I want' was 'I have, sort of'. Glinting hints of my own mortality began to show up when I was 17. Bright silver hairs appeared in a patch on the right side of my hairline. They were a different texture to the rest of my hair – aggressively springy as opposed to passive-aggressively frizzy. I plucked them out with a tweezers one evening in the bathroom as my sister brushed her teeth beside me, pausing to say, 'Pull out one grey and ten will come to the funeral.' I answered, 'Well, those ten will be wearing black so that's fine.' She lisped back, through quite a lot of toothpaste, 'That's such a stupid thing to say.' Maybe so, but the whole premise was introduced by her – the actual idea of a funeral service being held on my head for one hair, a service attended by ten other hairs – that was all her, and that was stupid too. I suppose we were a pair of stupid girls getting ready for bed in rural Ireland in 1998.

Now I am the age of Christ and there are plenty more

greys peeping out from under my crown of thorns. I make sure to get a single process colour once every six weeks, in dark brown for my sins. Now that I was choosing to dye my entire head of brown hair grey, my natural grey would surely blend in. I could disrupt my premature greyness with an even more premature greyness! Talk about beating the system!

My mother has iron-grey hair with some streaks of stubborn black. She used to get it coloured and the decision to stop doing so was much discussed at home. As her roots expanded down her head during the transition, she told me darkly, 'Other women resent me for this, you know.'

'Like who?' I asked.

She answered enigmatically. 'No one woman specifically.'

My mother is not yet 60, which is generally a lot younger than most of my peers' parents. Sometimes I ask strangers at parties how old their parents are so that I can tell them how young mine are. I'm always pleased when people exclaim, 'Wow – they are so young!' It's a pretty intense thing to boast about. Once when I did the trick on a new friend and he dutifully fell for it, telling me his parents were in their late 70s, he noted my smugness. 'Congratulations – your folks will probably be around longer than mine.' I was careful not to ask my usual follow-up questions about his parents' smoking habits and whether or not they owned a jet ski. I silently slid the rest of my survey back into my folder marked 'How long left? Other people's parents vs my parents'.

I like the idea of going grey. There is an honesty to it. Dying the grey hairs brown was akin to lying about my age, which is something I never want to do. My peers Taylor Swift and Miley Cyrus don't lie about their age, so why should I? That said, some very cool people do lie about their age. Frida Kahlo was born in 1907 but gave her year of birth as 1910 because that was the year the Mexican Revolution began and she felt she was not truly born until then. The Irish Republic declared its independence from Great Britain in January 1919. If I claimed that as my birth year it would make me pretty extraordinary, don't you think? Here I am, almost 100 years old, tweeting my outrage about various topics and eating ramen burgers; in other words, staying relevant.

That was another bonus, grey hair was on point, on fleek, bae as fuuuck. The coolest girls in my new neighbourhood, East Harlem, had dyed grey hair and they looked fantastic! For once, I would have a hairstyle that was actually cool. The realisation that every woman who looked good with dyed grey hair just happened to be Latina gave me pause. But not for long! I booked an appointment with a student hairdresser and dreamed of a silvery answer to all my troubles.

I entered the hair salon feeling buoyant. No longer would I fear becoming one of those old ladies who wear their glossy chestnut ringlets in pink ribbons, only to turn around quickly, shocking the people behind them with their wizened 90-year-old face and giggling at the horror they've caused. I was ready to go grey, happily.

The colour instructor stood over me, crowding out her student as she inspected my head and delivered her verdict. 'Where you're at right now, the most you can hope for is like a sandy orange colour and we can lift it again a coupla weeks later, to get all the pigment out, and after that you can maybe go red, maybe go blonde. Grey? I doubt it, sweetie.'

Thus ended my attempts to become a truthful hipster and a Hollywood starlet and my mother rolled into one. And thus began my new quest, unintentionally and with a discount of 70% because it was the student's second time using bleach, to become … a Blonde.

Congrats! Your Soul
Is Confirmed

Soulcycle is an exercise class invented here in New York by two powerfully blonde women. I heard it called a 'spiritual cardio party'. I heard that Lady Gaga had her birthday party there. I heard that people weep after classes because they've connected to a universal force through cycling on stationary bicycles in the dark.

The price of the first class is discounted heavily, which shows confidence in the product – a belief that once you've tried it you will want more. You'll be back, forever chasing that high, peddling toward Nirvana on a bike stuck to the ground. I wondered. Then I reserved a class online and got an email back saying, 'Congrats! Your SOUL is confirmed'.

You can imagine my relief. I was never totally sold on the idea that souls exist, but now I had an email from a multimillion-dollar corporation confirming that souls *do* exist, and I have one.

As I walked toward the studio the night of my first Soulcycle session, I realised I was starving. Right when that realisation occurred I found myself outside Vanessa's Dumplings. Isn't it funny how planets align and the universe catches you right when you need it to? Vanessa was the constellation I needed, her dumplings the stars. I hadn't eaten in probably three hours and you know how people sometimes faint if they push themselves too hard? I couldn't have that, not in Soulcycle, my body could not fail me as my spirit was elevating! So I thought I would have something light – perhaps a little bowl of broth to keep me going. I'm not sure how it happened, perhaps there were some translation difficulties between the waiter and myself, but somehow I ended up eating twelve shrimp dumplings and a sesame pancake the size of my face.

I felt uncomfortably full as I waited to sign in at reception, which was sleek and white like the lobby of any number of hotels I cannot afford to stay in. Soulcycle sell their own brand of clothing: gold leggings and mint-green T-shirts covered in bicycle wheel and pineapple motifs. I wanted those clothes immediately. I wished they were mine. This keeps happening to me in New York. I see a thing and I want it.

There's a sign on the wall with a list of acceptable behaviour in the studio, for example:

Number 2: No talking because that distracts the spiritual folks beside you.

'Spiritual folks' is not how I would describe the hard-bodied finance guys milling around, talking in that loud tone of empty camaraderie they have with one another. When I hear 'spiritual folks' I picture those sweetie-pie Hare Krishna's and the too-dense desserts they insist on making, or the elderly nun who taught me German in first year. I imagined Sister Deutsch shushing me with her spindly fingers as she got lost in house music.

Number 4: Do your laundry – we ride close together so we can feel each other's energy – that being said your neighbour does not want to feed off your odour.

I immediately resented the phrase 'feed off your odour' because I had never heard it before and now I knew it would stay in my head for years to come. It would possibly replace a phrase I love, a phrase like … oh dear Lord, I can't think of it now. See, that's just what happened! It better not have been 'What's good for the goose is good for the gander'. It couldn't be, I used that this morning in Wholefoods when that man reached across me to get the carton of eggs I was about to take. It was a pick-up line of sorts, one that he failed to pick up on, or possibly even hear.

Sometimes I'm not sure if I've said something aloud or just to myself.

The odour reference also worried me because I didn't want anyone to feed off my odour or vice-versa. I wasn't sure which was worse, until two seconds later when I decided that, of course, the latter is far worse. Luckily, a beautiful girl model distracted me from my grim musings by handing me a pair of clip-in cycling shoes and showing me around the locker rooms. As I followed her shining, swinging ponytail around the luxurious shower rooms, I began to get suspicious.

There were white fluffy towels, fancy moisturisers, safety razors – classic rich people things. I asked the beautiful child about the price of a regular class; there was no mention of it on the Soulcycle website –but that doesn't mean it's a free service for the community. The little girl told me it costs $34 and $3 for shoes. I said (you're going to love this), 'Wow – do the teachers cycle for you?' She replied sweetly, 'Nobody can do Soulcycle for you, but Isobel will be there with you – really *with* you – she is awesome – she is a fitness instructor, a DJ and a guru.' That impressed me. In school I had regular meetings with a guidance counsellor and none of those three careers were ever an option, let alone all three together. God Bless America.

The changing room walls boasted huge magazine interviews with the company's founders, who discussed how successful they are and how addictive their product is. I pulled on my cycling shoes, surely a member of the holy trinity of ugly shoes. (Bowling shoes naturally join them, and those hideous little climbing slippers complete the picture.) At a glance – nothing more than a glance is permitted in a changing room – no peeps, gazes or stares allowed – I noticed that the other women were all between 18 and 40. Size 18–40, you guys. Psych! J.K.J.K.! Gotcha. I mean they ranged in *age* from 18–40. I locked my bag away and filed silently into the studio, just another member of the plodding herd clip-clopping along.

The studio was dark and felt like a cinema right before the film begins – the same sense of anticipation, just a sweatier smell and no buttery popcorn. Rows and rows of bikes were truly packed with bodies. It was almost as if they were trying to make as much money as poss— oh no! I beg your pardon; I suppose it's like the rules say, Soulcycle just really prefers when people feel one another's energy. There were candles lighting and loud music playing – incredibly loud music.

The only other time I've heard music that loud is from my headphones when I'm depressed and trying to blot my mind out. A sylph was handing out earplugs but I declined. I wanted to find my soul like they promised and what if my vital force happened to be whispering around a Lana del Rey song? I didn't want two little pieces of yellow foam to block my path to enlightenment. I got on my assigned bike and clipped in with some effort. I knew I should do that because I had watched what everyone else did. When you are new, you have to watch people and copy them. I seem to do that a lot.

The instructor/DJ/guru took up her spot on a raised platform. She looked like a future human, perfectly proportioned with a successful haircut, wearing space-age fabric and a face-mic. She yelled a greeting to everyone to the class, referring to us as her '8.30s' – asking how all her 8.30s were, and if there were any beginners in her 8.30s. I raised my hand and she spotted me though the gloom. 'Welcome!' she shouted. 'You're not gonna remember anything that came before your first Soulcycle.'

I was impressed. The class would wipe my past, acting in the same way a lobotomy would, or really any severe brain injury.

As we began to warm up, I had to make a snap decision. Did I want to remember anything that happened in my past, or was I better off forgetting? Here is a list.

THINGS I'D LIKE TO REMEMBER:

1. The look in my granddad's gimlet eyes right as he plotted a prank phone call to his friend.

2. The answers to my Visa extra secure questions – too many times those devilish questions have locked me out of an important online purchase of old wedding dresses (don't even ask).

3. The way my toddler nephew hugged me out of nowhere when we were kneeling on the kitchen floor playing with plastic dinosaurs.

4. How to make roast garlic and butternut squash soup.

5. My friends Kevin and Elna keeping me a seat at a fundraising show. I couldn't find them and was wandering around a packed room with increasing anxiety, until I saw them. They both extended their arms in a 'we're over here' gesture and I felt my shoulders relax as I realised *there they are, my friends.*

THINGS I'D RATHER FORGET:

1. The time I was staying with my brother and his girlfriend and I thought they had left so I went snooping in their room. I was just looking at some socks in a drawer when I noticed in the wardrobe mirror that his girlfriend was wide awake in bed, looking at me in a horrified way.

2. The way I bombed so hard on a British TV show the crew started packing up the set while I was still performing.

3. Various texts I've sent to people about themselves.

4. All of the fake tan choices I've made.

5. The number of promises I've made to myself and not kept in every sphere of my life including and not limited to physical, mental, psychic and sexual.

As it turns out, that chart is moot, because my memory remained intact, even after a spinning class with a lot of press-ups and some weights. I even remember how the teacher had a funny way of counting the beat. She would grunt sexily for the 'one two three' then shout throatily 'five shix sheven' and sort of moan/scream the final 'eight'. I remember being glad of two things – the dark, and the fact that I was in the second row. There were mirrors covering the front wall. It is one thing to fail at something, it's another thing completely to watch yourself failing from 14 different angles.

I failed at Soulcycle. I could do the cycle part, but not the soul. People around me were shrieking with joy when the bass dropped, or when the instructor/DJ/guru called out 'How are you 8.30s?'

I cursed Vanessa and her delicious sesame pancakes. I thought, perhaps I wasn't fully engaged because it was a tough workout and I feared I might vomit dumplings all over the Lycra-clad cherub in front of me. Another reason could have been that the Soulcycle experience contains within it almost every element of my longest-running bad dreams. Strangers' asses close to my face, clattering self-doubt, shouted orders, excessive cardio, rising anxiety about what is going to happen, weird smells. The only thing missing, the final element that would make the nightmare complete? Well – that would be a fish. I would know I was having a nightmare and wake up screaming for sure if there was a large fish nearby and it touched me. At one point I glanced at my neighbour, fully expecting to see a huge pollock lazily keeping the beat side-saddle – possibly reaching his fin out to rub up the length of my arm. There was no spinning pollock, just an intensely tech-looking guy towelling sweat away from eyes that stayed fixed on some invisible spot ahead.

Flourishing under
the Male Gays

I'm in a small kitchen two blocks away from the last stop on the Q train, it smells like caramel and clean laundry and I'm talking to Tom Moulton – full-time paediatric haematologist oncologist, part-time baker. 'Soda bread, scones, ginger snaps, oatmeal cookies and,' he pauses, 'cashew nut brittle, if I have time.' He's making vittles to raise funds for St Pat's for All – a small St Patrick's Day parade founded by his husband Brendan Fay that takes place annually in Sunnyside, Queens – an alternative to the New York City St Patrick's Day parade that marches up Manhattan's Fifth Avenue that, in 1992, banned gay people from marching under an identifying banner.

I decided to write about that big parade for *The Irish Times* – partially because the ban struck me as unfair and outdated, but also because the parade was the biggest and oldest one in the city, and it represents Irishness. I liked the idea that it was started by a bunch of Irishmen serving in the British army who found a little pocket of freedom in Manhattan in 1762. They marched, they sang Irish songs, they wore green, which was banned back home. They expressed themselves freely in this new land. Over the years, as the Irish community in America grew bigger and stronger, the parade did too. An organisation called The Ancient Order of Hibernians kept it going and still organises it to this day. The parade is indeed a mighty sight – a serious affair, not a parade in the sense of a fun celebration, it feels more like a demonstration of power. There is music – marching music, pipe bands and drums. The banners are simple, bordering on somber. Each county is represented and there are soldiers, police and firefighters all in uniform, as well as columns of men in dark suits and sashes. These acres of white men pause outside St Patrick's Cathedral to be blessed by another old white man in a pointy hat. Keeping it 'traditional' is hugely important to the organisers, they do not approve of floats or green beads or flashing shamrock earrings or, you know, people who aren't heterosexual.

Reaching the Fifth Avenue parade committee is tricky. I see that they are having a function to honour their Grand Marshal so I phone their office to ask if I can go. A voice replies, 'Absolutely not. Why would we want you lurkin' around, Ma'am?' This year they are under more pressure than ever before to lift the ban, to stop discriminating. Politicians are refusing to march with them, sponsors are threatening to pull out, the American and the Irish media talk of little else when it comes to the big day.

I want to talk to them about the ban, and also about what being Irish in America feels like to them. Being Irish American is different to being Irish, I can see that much. It's an identity all its own, made up of nostalgia for a place that no longer exists, politics that are both nationalistic and aspirational and, of course, that mystery meat I tasted for the first time at a food truck at the Kansas City Irish Festival – corned beef. The committee is annoyed with the press, and so I never get my interview and am left to figure out Irish-Americanness in other ways.

I do talk to Brendan Fay and the St Pat's for All committee. Every Saturday morning in the months leading up to the parade, they meet in Molly Blooms, an Irish bar in Sunnyside, and drink tea and try to figure out the logistics on the portable toilets, step dancers and puppets. One volunteer explains that there's a huge warehouse of damaged puppets out in Brooklyn, a sort of puppet rescue facility, and the committee takes a truckload each year to distribute to the kids in the neighbourhood, so they too can be part of the parade. Queens is the most ethnically diverse urban area in the world, and the idea of this multi-ethnic cast of children holding busted-up puppets aloft in a celebration of Ireland is just so beautiful, it makes me do what I often do when things get emotional. I start laughing. Fay steps in, a small, bright-eyed man who, when he looks at you, really looks at you, 'To say "you do not belong" is such a hurtful and harmful message. All of this talk about Ireland of the welcomes, we're meant to be known for that, so to me St Pat's for All is almost restoring something the Irish were known for – being welcoming – it's a special human quality and people need it.'

Acceptance, inclusion and love – these can change a person's life. I think about what I have needed in my life and in my work and where and how I've gotten it. A community that has supported and bolstered me, despite my not being one of them, is the gay community. Look, I'm about to go balls to the wall for gay people, although it is probably not cool to do so because of course sexuality is just one aspect of a person. I am all set to paint all gay people with the same brush, an adoring one, an appreciative one, but the same one nonetheless and for that I apologise. Now I'm going to go ahead and say it, loud and proud. Gay people are the best. I love gay people!

Being gay is not a choice; one reason I believe that is because gay people say so. The other reason is that, if it *were* a choice, I would totally be gay.

I can't recall the first time I heard the word gay, but it was almost certainly in school and definitely used as an insult, a slur. In 1980s Ireland, nobody sat me down and explained that heterosexuality is just one type of sexuality, there are others and they are all normal. My mother described gay women as 'raging lesbians' or maybe she said 'raving lesbians'. I couldn't tell how much of that was a joke; it left me with the impression that lesbians were always either being furious or dancing frantically to trance music in a field outside of Leeds. From what I understand now, lesbians are doing neither. Raves? Nope. And why would lesbians be furious? They get to be with women and, watch out for the giant brush again, women are the greatest.

Women ask me questions and listen to my answers and can even tell what I'm actually trying to say underneath those answers. Women always have an envelope when you need one and their hair smells so lovely. They are resilient and kind. Women manage to be simultaneously soft and strong. They express themselves thoughtfully, which may seem hesitant, but is infinitely preferable to domineering. They wear pretty glinting earrings and make sly, hilarious jokes. They can grow, deliver and sustain another human being using only their bodies. Thank God for jewel-coloured fabrics on warm summer skin and fingernails painted light blue. And lesbian couples get to *both be women*!

I love my women friends so much that I wish I could be *in* love with them. I marvel at their smarts, their beauty and their kindness. I ask my lesbian friends if they think I could possibly be one of them. I explain that I adore women, that my relationships with women are the most meaningful of my life and somehow the most romantic. I would dearly love a wife, like some of them have. I picture my wife and I in matching outfits, reading one another's minds, knowing just what cramps feel like. I could share with my partner an innate understanding of the difficulty of keeping your head up in a world run by men. How about it? I ask. My friends are kind and patient as they explain that unless I'm sexually attracted to women, I'm not gay.

I plead with them that I was raised in a Catholic society with all the simmering misogyny and homophobia that entails, and perhaps that's why I'm just not *free* enough to be gay. I say maybe this hetero thing is just a phase I'm going through. They look doubtful. Lots of them were brought up that way too, or worse, but they never stepped aboard the D train. Or if they did, they realised quickly it was the wrong train and got off at the next station, Sapphic Town.

Me, I'm stuck on the D all the way to Straightsville. Reluctantly, through no fault of my own, or my parents', or the society I grew up in, I'm sexually attracted to men. I can't help it – their arrogance, their smell, their maleness – that's what I want in my bed. It's so annoying! Some days, I wish there was some sort of reverse conversion therapy to change me into a successful, happy lesbian. The only problem is, even if it existed for straight to gay, conversion therapy is a crazy pseudo-science that doesn't work, so that's that. I've got to come to terms with my heterosexuality. All I have is this precious closeness with my darling women and of course, my gay, gay men.

It grosses me out when straight girls talk about their gay male friends as if they are accessories, and vice versa. My relationships with gay men have been real and important ever since my first one when I was 15 years old. Someone needs to document the torrid and tender nature of the friendships between chubby teenage girls and gawky gay boys, they are surely a sacred thing. They have an intimacy all of their own, and they are a rehearsal for intimacies to come. One of my earliest confidantes was a gay boy, a friend of my older brother's. Paul would phone me every Thursday evening and we would talk in low urgent voices for hours at a time. Thursday was a quiet night in my house – I was usually babysitting my sleeping sisters while my parents visited their parents. Paul had a girlfriend, but I knew he loved boys. He knew I knew but we never mentioned it, unknowingly echoing the 'don't ask, don't tell' policy employed by the US military at the time, except with less implied hatred, more kinship. I was beyond besotted with a boy in Paul's school. It was a truly impossible dream, but Paul would ask about my crush and I'd breathlessly tell him every detail. 'I saw him on the train on my way to get my braces tightened,' I would lisp. 'He was wearing rugby shorts and I think he saw me but I'm not sure, anyway I phoned his house and hung up three times before dinner.'

I found out years later that over the course of our friendship, Paul was having a love affair with a boy in his class, a 'straight' boy who had sworn him to secrecy. We were both trapped, both longing. Paul was the only one who made that crazy adolescent journey with me. Perhaps he comforted me through my melancholy fantasies because he had his own, or perhaps we were just lucky to find each other – we were *anam cairde*, soul friends.

It's hard to say just what it is that I love about my gay male friends, without sounding trite, or stereotyping them. I guess I just I adore their fashion sense and bitchy repartee! No, no, that is not it at all, although there is a wit and elegance that I find in only them. I once sat in the back of a cab between two flirting men and felt like I'd died and gone to heaven. These were two greats, at the top of their game, and the dialogue was unburdened and thrilling to hear.

At some point in their lives, many gay men and women have been made to feel less than normal. They are often seen as 'other' and I wonder if this injustice leads to them being perhaps more understanding and humane than the heterosexual population. It certainly seems to me that when a gay man looks at me, he can actually see me. The connection is clear and untrammelled by hormones. Similar to how it is with women, there is less assessing, more accepting and the connection I feel is to the person. Being drawn to a person is hugely down to the personality of that individual, of course, but the common denominator in many of my most important friendships, the one that bolsters me and gives me agency, is that they are with gay men.

Not a whole lot of gay men do stand-up comedy, I suspect for the same reasons not a lot of women do. All too often, stand-up becomes a blunt instrument. The parts of comedy that I love – the spontaneity, nuance and honesty – are often bludgeoned to oblivion by arrogance, shouting and machismo. In my work, I don't profile people that come to shows or read my writing, but it's impossible not to notice a steady stream of hand-holding men with great hair in the front rows and impossible to ignore their murmurs of approval when I launch into an impression of Addison de Witt. Since I started doing stand-up ten years ago, gay men have been there for me, getting my meaning, laughing me on. I am grateful for this support, for it makes me think I must be doing something right. Gay people have a history of championing women who speak up and artists who don't exactly fit in. I hope to be both of those things and their belief in my work helps me to keep trying. It sounds self-important, I know, but as a wise man once said, 'We all come into this world with our little egos equipped with individual horns. If we don't blow them, who else will?'

To round out my St Patrick's Day story for the newspaper, I go along to a reception honoring the two Grand Marshals of St Pat's for All. I write about the party hosted by the Irish Consul General on the 50th floor of a beautiful building in midtown. Tom Duane is one of the grand marshals, he looks like a clean-shaven Santa, and chuckles like him too. Proud of his family heritage, all four grandparents were Irish immigrants to America, Duane was elected to the New York State Senate in 1998. He became the Senate's first openly gay and first openly HIV-positive member. Duane was arrested many times for protesting at the Fifth Avenue parade and was among the first politicians to support Fay's parade. 'Now, they're all at it!' he says, a grin ruining the credibility of his attempted eye-roll.

It's true, nobody knows it yet but the political and financial pressure on the larger parade means that 2014 is the final year the ban will hold. Nobody knows this yet either but in just over a year's time Ireland will become the first country in the world to legalise same-sex marriage through popular vote. The other St Pat's for All Grand Marshal, Terry McGovern, a softly spoken human rights lawyer with copper-coloured hair, gives a short speech that honours her mother, who worked at the World Trade Centre and died there on 11 September 2001. 'She was the first one to introduce me to the concept of human rights, she had an amazing sense of humour and would have been so happy that I'm here tonight.'

Malachy McCourt sings 'Will You Go, Lassie, Go', and pretty much everyone joins in. Then it's the turn of a Brooklyn man who could be an extra from *The Sopranos*, but he plays the fiddle like an angel, specifically, an angel from Sligo. He closes his eyes as the notes of the reel whirl and slip through the assembled crowd who whoop and tap as the city glitters beneath them. St Pat's for All is back on the Sunnyside streets the following week, with puppets and dancers and rainbow flags flying. These are people hoping for change but not waiting for it, inviting everyone around them to join in, reminding them that all are welcome.

Last night I introduced my friend Kevin to a guy I'm seeing. We went for food together, low pressure. Kevin and I were going on the way we do, not in-jokey exactly just being together in a way that is so comfortable and fun I wish I could bottle the alchemy for blue days. I looked at my date across the table and wondered crossly why he wasn't joining in the fun. He was frowning into his phone, replying to an email about work. I noticed that muscle men have, the one in their cheek that flexes when they clench their jaw. So hot. I knew that of course he couldn't join in, because he didn't speak the language. I also knew that I'd be going home with him anyway.

Men!

Movie Roles for
Your Girl Higgins

My agent contacted me recently in what I now know to be a butt dial. My plaintive exclamations of, 'Hello, hello? It's so great to hear from you – it's been so long – not that I'm accusing you of, oh anyway, what news?!' were met with static at first, then a muffled conversation I probably should not have been privy to. My agent was having coffee with my manager and lawyer and they were discussing my lack of movie appearances. In between fits of laughter and mouthfuls of cream cake, they lamented my unreliable hair and my ability to do only three accents: Cobh, Midleton and Cork. 'She keeps sending me gifts!' shrieked my lawyer. 'And I'm like – honey – just get a contract! For anything!' Right before I hung up the phone, I heard a triple high-five and what sounded like two of these professional women bumping tummies in some kind of victory gesture.

This call and meeting are fictional; my manager and agent have never even met each other. (That is possibly not great. What if one of them thinks I want to be on British panel shows just so I can set fire to the sets and another thinks I want to get married and quit the business entirely and only by meeting they will discover that I'm exactly half way between both of those impulses?) If they did meet they would not eat cream cakes. They are too grown up and in control of themselves for cream cakes and that is why I need them. As for my lawyer, you're not going to believe this but she is a *he*. That's right, I got one of those rare *male* lawyers. He's a bit skittish but coming along nicely. And there is never any menstrual blood on any of my legal papers, so that's nice.

The person missing from my team is a casting director. These are the people who decide which actor gets to play which role. Even in their own lives they cast people all day long. Listen carefully to LA-based women dressed in expensively casual clothes and you will hear them casting constantly. 'You, be my waiter, get me Rooibos tea! And you, there, with the red hair! You will be my quirky best friend. OK – tell me not to call the guy, but then you call him – but put on a funny voice while you're doing it!' I have decided to employ a casting director and explain that I can't do auditions because I'm too self-important. She will understand who I am as an actor and in which roles I will excel, with the following guidelines I have written to help her.

Height: 5'7½"
Weight: Varies According to Mental Weather
Hair: See 'Weight'
Eyes: Murky Blue

Looks
— Exhausted Nurse
— Tired Wife
— Put-upon Girlfriend
— Sad Widow
— Secretly Pleased Widow
— Antony from Antony and The Johnsons
— Scatty but Well-Meaning Civil Servant
— Pale Crime Victim
— Brunette
— School Teacher, Only if the Movie is Set Before 1990
— Inexplicably Blonde Brunette
— Sick Person in Hospital/at Home
— Rural Driving Instructor, as Long as I Don't Have to Drive Because I Can't

Accents
Wonderful range of regional accents covering almost the entire span of south-east County Cork.

Skills

Things I can do simultaneously

— Hold a Baby on One Hip and Stir a Pot
— Eat and Talk
— Have Sex and Text

Things I can do one-by-one (N.B. *not* simultaneously)

— Walk
— Apply Eyeliner
— Drop Down Low and Sweep the Floor with It

Voice-overs

— A Gruff Man in the 1930s
— A Silly Youngish Girl
— A Gender-Neutral Wheedling Misfit

Suitable Roles

1. Maeve Is Kindness

It may seem difficult to make kindness, the state or quality of being kind, into a character in a movie but that's just the kind of work we pay writers very little to do. Here is a head start for them, in the form of some sample scenes.

Scene I: A curly haired woman (played by Maeve) tries to enter the driver's compartment on a busy train, mistaking it for the restroom. She yanks at the locked door handle and shoulders the door angrily before realising her foolishness. Embarrassed, she quickly makes her way back through the carriage, making eye contact with a teenage boy as she goes. The boy saw her gaffe and is doing all he can to suppress his laughter. The woman shapes her fingers into a gun and pretends to shoot herself in the head, thereby giving him permission to laugh in that honking, rasping way of teenage boys.

Scene II: (explanatory flashback) A curly haired four-year-old with a tummy bug lies in bed sadly. She listens to the ruckus of children downstairs and wishes she were part of it. The day stretches out. After a lunch of lemonade flattened with hot water she hears her grandmother's voice and sits up, hoping she won't be forgotten. The grandmother (played by Maeve, using prosthetics and make-up obviously) walks up the stairs in a brisk, practical way that makes the child realise she has come to visit her especially. Having an adult all to herself is an unprecedented thrill, but this afternoon she is too tired to show off. The grandmother doesn't mind that the child is quiet and gives her a book to read, about a duck that can brush his teeth and hold down an office job. Then the grandmother sits at the end of the bed and rubs the child's feet until she falls asleep.

I already pitched 'Kindness' to the head of a Hollywood studio. He thundered up from his leather chair and furiously stubbed out a cigar, yelling: 'A goddamn footrub?! I want grand gestures. Did the train crash? Did the old dame give that kid a kidney? No? Then I'm not interested! You come in my office sellin' me a finger gun, some screwy duck and a goddamn footrub? That ain't nothing!'

I got on my feet and I set him straight: 'I'm telling you, Boss, you're wrong, the small stuff is where it's at, right there in those tiny moments that go unnoticed by most when one creature sees what another creature needs – a look, a touch, a word, a lift – and simply gives it to them, that's kindness!'

The studio head nodded then, a broken-down bear with something to think about.

2. Maeve Is a Bat

Students of motion picture history will be familiar with a little franchise about men dressed like bats. The *Batman* movies, and there are many of them – too many to count while my Internet has been cut off – are enormously successful and have made stars out of many a chisel-jawed actor. I will be next. You ask me how, I say it's simple – I may not be able to play a man, but I can certainly play a bat. I know all about them, because I am meticulous in my research for any role.

Bats are little tiny mice that can fly and are powered by batteries, hence their name. When they are running low on charge, they emit a high beeping noise. Despite what smoke alarms would have you believe they actually stole that idea from bats, not the other way around.

To recharge, bats must do two things. The tired ones must plug themselves into a little cave, it's not clear how, for about 20 minutes. Then, they must really relax. No screens, no crazy-making arguments with co-parents about who spends more time with the batlettes – just dozing. These bat naps perk them right up and off they fly, slapping each other on their spiny backs, saying things like, 'Barbara, you look ten years younger!'

I wouldn't be the first great Irish actor to play a bat. Ever heard of Dracula? Sure you have. Well, he was a bat! I chatted to Jonathan Rhys Meyers about his time living with Carlow's bat community as preparation for his TV role in which he plays that very bat (Dracula). 'They're cool,' said the handsomely laconic actor, wings loose and broad as he nibbled on a moth, discarding the head. Everyone watching in the central Dublin hotel immediately copied him. The waiter told me later that they ran out of moths that afternoon. Don't worry, I reported that waiter for gossiping.

One teenage bat I interviewed for this piece, who declined to give his name, had this to say. 'We don't give a fuck what non-flying creatures think of us, 'specially mice, man.' So you see, Jonathan Rhys Meyers is right, bats *are* cool. They are not scary or bad. I will change how Hollywood and therefore the world views and treats bats. Their reputation will only get cooler after my tour de force in a high-budget romance action movie. That's right, my character will fall in love and also do martial arts.

3. Maeve Is a Boxer

Typecasting, I know. Many people mistake me for a boxer when I strut around my East Harlem neighbourhood. 'Put 'em up, Mami!' they shout and I shake my head. 'No, no, Edmundo; you can't handle my left hook.' And we all laugh and clink our seltzer bottles together and settle down for a game of dominoes instead. I took boxing classes in the past but they took place in a dance studio. You may ask, 'What is boxing but a dance with punches?' Great question. Why don't you ask Lucille and Roberta, my fists? Sorry, please accept my apologies for that aggressive outburst. I was slipping into character.

You see, every true star needs a boxing movie and I am no different. Myself, Robert de Niro, Hilary Swank; do we not all twinkle in the same galaxy, that far off one, just beyond your reach? We do indeed. With that in mind, my boxing movie will be based on a proven box office hit. As we say in the boxing world, 'If it ain't broke, don't fix it, unless you're breakin' a nose or fixin' a fight.' Using an old idea means we don't even have to pay a writer, thereby saving $30 that can be redirected to catering.

Boxing Movie Remakes for Maeve to Star In

Golden Boy (1939)
Logline: Despite his musical talent, Joe Bonaparte wants to be a boxer.

My character, Josephine Bonaparte (no, not that one!), is a lithe recorder player who is almost up to grade 3 level. She is good enough to try out for the church's musical group, as the person who toots the note the choir needs to start on. However, on her way there a bully takes her recorder and when she tells the priest about this he doesn't believe her. She boxes him in the face, actually she does Muay Thai, kicking him in the solar plexus too, and this was well before Muay Thai was even a thing in Ireland. After that, the wowed choir sings outside shopping centres to fund Josephine's trip to the Olympics where she fights a Chechen man who, unbeknownst to anyone, is suffering badly with jaundice. She defeats 'Golden Boy' and becomes welterweight champion of the world.

The Boxer (1997)
Logline: Danny Flynn gets out of jail after taking the rap for the IRA

Danielle Flynn takes the rap for everything. Much like the actor playing her (me, I'm the actor) Danielle would do anything to avoid conflict. So when her sister steals a padded bra from Marks and Spencer, the naturally busty Danielle steps in. She serves three hard hours in Mountjoy. After that, she's back on the streets, and ready to crumble. That's right, she is a boxer *and* a baker. She punches flour bags and spars with sugar cane. Her confectionery draws

Catholics and Protestants alike into her wee bakery on the Falls Road. Nancy Meyers directs.

Southpaw (2015)

At the time of writing, I have yet to see this Jake Gyllenhaal Oscar vehicle. I long to, of course, having seen the trailers every time I sneak into the movie theatre ten blocks away to 'look for my little daughter'. That's a ruse, of course. I'm looking for my hero and I find him each time; up on the big screen, my boy Jake, all grown up. All filled out. All pent up. Lord have mercy! What a man. He is the trifecta of sexiness – a boxer, a widower and an addict. I aspire to ape his greatness in my role in *Southpaw II: Further South*. I will bulk up for the role, that's no problem. I will play an alcoholic widow; people will love that, especially guys! My puffy cut-up face and determination to get my daughter out of care will endear the public to me and I too shall win an Oscar, thereby evening the playing field between myself and my son and my husband, Jake Gyllenhaal.

There you have it, I've cleaned up my side of the street pretty nicely. Now all that's left to do is to set up a casting session to find my dream casting director. So far my criteria are that they be six-foot-one and tons of fun, so if you know anyone, please do refer them to my agent. I don't have her contact details right now, she appears to have moved office and/or retired and/or passed away.

Charlotte Vale's Mother

Once upon a time, this busy little fool lost all of her cards. I was about to head out the door for a day of meetings when I looked in my stupid little wallet and saw that they were missing. I knew at once with a painful clarity, the kind felt by a lazy husband when he realises those underpants in the laundry basket are not his, that my precious ones had strayed because of sheer carelessness on my part. It was my neglect, my distracted manner that caused the cards to wander. I lay on the ground in my bedroom, dead still – for how long I cannot say. Outside the window, children laughed and birds chirped. Inside, resting on the wooden floor with its eyes closed as the light changed and shadows grew, was my head. And inside that head, accusations churned and slammed.

The Screeching Voice, sounding chillingly like Charlotte Vale's mother in *Now, Voyager*, demanded that I answer the following questions, which I did, as best I could.

Voice: Are you surprised that this has happened? It's not the first time – is it, Maeve?

Maeve: No. It happens all the time because I'm such a loser clown.

Voice: You are indeed, a total loser clown. Thinking you are so great because you bought a green juice earlier, but you're a simple country mouse that can't do the most basic of things. Imagine if you owned a home – you'd lose that too! Not that there is any prospect of that happening because you are so wickedly lazy and poor, isn't that right?

Maeve: Yes. Totally. Also, if I owned a home I'd decorate it badly because I have poor taste and little patience for aesthetics. Oh dear.

Voice: And whom would you live with, even? In this ugly imaginary home you can never afford? No pets, no MAN. Would you live alone like the odd old witch you are, or perhaps you'd still live with flatmates! Why – you're an absolute tragedy! You're almost 40!!

Maeve: But I'm only 32 … and I quite like living with other people …

Voice: Ah yes, grin and bear it – you and your lies – maybe that's why you look so old! And another thing, don't you even remember how difficult it was to get your New York State non-driver's ID? The one you've just lost?

I sank deeper then, into a remembrance of an interminable day in April spent at the Department of Motor Vehicles office in downtown Manhattan. Long lines of people shifted crossly in rows of plastic chairs as the wait stretched into hours. All the sockets were boarded up so nobody could charge their phones, thus doubling the anxiety of the assembled New Yorkers.

A man with a high ponytail sat beside me and asked if I knew whether or not switching back and forth between airplane mode and regular mode helped conserve the battery. 'I'm down to 11% and I'm number 421,' he said, his eyes darting about desperately. I shrugged and listened to a podcast sped up by half, hoping that would conserve enough battery to allow me to watch some shouting goat videos afterwards. The ponytailed man simmered as I blissed out with my device. Two hours later, my phone died too and I attempted to re-engage him in conversation. 'Did you ever see those videos of goats that shout like men?' I asked. He shrugged a revenge shrug, slow and deliberate, thrilled with the chance to shut me down as I had shut him down.

I had filled out lots of paperwork that day, promised two different people in uniform that I was a legal alien, and had my photo taken by a very nice man who advised me to 'Tuck my chin in, but not down'. The wait was totally worth it, I was very proud of my non-driver's ID with its big New York stamp and a hologram of my head on it, clear and floating in the right hand corner. Now, of course, I had lost it. My face, smiling forever in its transparent prison, trodden on by big dirty boots and spiked by cheap stilettoes somewhere on a Brooklyn street. *Unless*, I thought, *somebody finds it, and sends it to me – after all, my address is on the card! And just two weeks ago I found a set of keys on the street and posted them to the gym on one of the key-rings. Surely karma might ...* I was interrupted by the Screeching Voice.

Voice: Oh yes indeed, aren't you the kind girl? Tell me the real reason you sent those keys back, you desperate maniac!

Maeve: Umm just so they'd find their owner?

Voice: You can't fool me – I know all of your thoughts!

Maeve: Well for a split second, when I saw that they belonged to someone who worked out at the Harlem YMCA, I imagined having a mixed-race baby with a wonderful Ghanaian man. But I didn't put my name on the envelope or anything – returning those keys was totally pure in its motivation, I ... I ...

Voice: You, Madame, are a psychopath! And now what are you going to do, all alone with no bank-cards? You know how impossible it is to replace them. Unless you can remember your passwords for your online banking ... can you?

Maeve: No. No I can't. I can't remember them and I can't remember where I wrote them down. Sometimes I can get into the system but when they ask for that second 'verified' password, I crumble. I am terrible at the most basic ways of being an adult.

Voice: *(laughing and laughing)* You should kill yourself!

Maeve: Oh, that's new. Hmmm.

Eventually I sat up and got dressed, using the clothes lying nearest to me on the floor. I set off for the bank. The Screeching Voice piped up along the way, critical of my reflection in a shop window, mocking a text message to a friend saying 'things are good' with a heart and a little monkey covering its mouth emoji.

I turn onto Church Avenue, past the DNA testing centre with its big sign saying 'Are you sure he's got your eyes?' The baby pictured has glowing sky-blue eyes; there is no doubt that he is not a human child, so the odds seem stacked against any potential baby-daddy. I walk by Bobby's Department Store, its windows crammed with knock-off tutus featuring a cross-eyed version of Elsa from *Frozen* and $9 rice cookers.

Dollar cabs toot their horns and swing in to pick up old ladies who stand with their hands on hips, yams and plantains double-bagged at their feet. The subway station is low and old, all oranges and browns with a wet, muddy floor. The doors swing open and a vague smell of bleach emerges, along with an ancient bearded man half-heartedly asking people for change. He ambles over to a large woman, the circle of her tummy smiling out from under her shirt, who is selling bed-sheets from a cardboard box for $6 apiece and they shake hands, they are friends. Some creature has rummaged through the trash bags outside Checkers Chicken, spilling their contents onto the path. I pick my way through the dirty little bone-yard on the kerb before I turn onto Flatbush Avenue.

I wonder do I live here, or do I live in my head?

The bank faces a Mens Top Fashion Shop, specialising in shining suits and pointy shoes. There is a Dunkin' Donuts next door and a lawyer's office above that, its neon signs flashing pink for immigration and blue for divorce. There's a long line for the single cashier window that's open, and I join it. I have a cheque to lodge for $125 and I'm pleased I've remembered to bring it along. Then I realise this will only bring my balance up to $32 and I'm less pleased.

A bank clerk works his way down the line, speaking to each person; one by one they shake their heads. I know what he is doing, and it annoys me. He's trying to make us leave the queue and do our business at the machines in the foyer. *Why is he working against his own future?* I think darkly. *By sending us towards the machines, he's helping them win.* I put in my headphones and when he asks me something I tell him crisply, 'I'm good, thank you.' He smiles and motions for me to remove my headphones; I find this immensely irritating but I do it. He has a soft African accent and a stammer that takes the form of a long pause before words while his mouth silently makes the shape of the word he's about to say.

'Tell me why you are here and I can help you.' I tell him I need to lodge a cheque and order a new card. His face lights up and he says, slowly, 'You can leave here today with a new card, Madame – it's not so difficult – you put in that cheque then come talk to me and I will introduce you to my co-worker and we will get you a new card.' He seems excited for me.

One corner of the bank has a small waiting area with six blue chairs in a row against a partition. There is a water cooler and a little counter with a coffee machine bearing the bank's logo and a smiley face with a speech bubble saying 'Help Yourself'. A security guard stands near the machine, looking out the window and humming to himself. A tall woman in thigh-high boots and leggings printed with the cosmos comes clattering in the door, swinging a tiger print handbag from one elbow, one hand clutching a paper bag from McDonald's. She is talking loudly on a glittery phone that is sandwiched between her studded pleather shoulder and a huge wig of shining copper curls. She snatches a polystyrene cup from the counter and sits beside me. 'Eh, eh,' she calls to the security man. 'You are missing the cream and sugar eh, come on now.' He nods gravely and walks off. The woman huffs and continues her phone conversation. 'Nah nah he and she are not together nah nah he a batty boy he just a batty boy I tell you now.' She continues in this vein, speaking so rapidly that the person on the other end of the call surely couldn't have time to respond. I wonder if there is anyone there at all.

The security man returns with a carton of half and half and a box of sugar and this giant ragdoll from the future doesn't miss a beat. Still chatting, she gets her coffee and strides back out of the bank, leaving behind a trail of sugar, napkins and spilled coffee.

I catch eyes with an old man leaning on a cane at the other end of the row and we both start to laugh. The security guard laughs too, but ruefully. He says, 'OK so you come in here for your morning coffee and you don't use the bank? OK – but you leave a mess? The way I was raised … that's not OK.' He is cleaning up the mess and shaking his head. I tell him I suspected there wasn't anyone on the phone; he agrees. 'She was frontin' but there's no need, I don't stop people if they want to get coffee. Come on now, it's cold today. Just don't leave such a mess, you know?'

The old man is called, he had signed in just ahead of me with large shaky handwriting, 'Peter'. The security guard and I talk about boxing. I ask him who would win, Ali or Tyson, if they were both in their prime. He says, 'You know that's interesting, because I'm Tyson's height but I'm Ali's build.' I don't disagree but I guess I look dubious because he quickly adds, 'Of course this winter I'm not in condition, on account of my injuries.' He gives me a business card for the gym he works at. I put it in my empty wallet as he tells me that true fighters are the most peaceful people he knows, because they deal with their feelings by actually feeling them, then letting them pass.

Some version of my name gets called to go sit in a cubicle with a bank manager called Hestor, a middle-aged man with a Caribbean lilt who smells amazing, clean and grown-up like lime and cigars. I want to say, 'You smell *so* good,' but I can't always say what I want. Last week on the train I said to a young boy, 'Hey, why didn't you skate home?' I said that because I thought he was holding a skateboard, but it was actually a plank of wood. He took out his headphones and I repeated it. 'Why didn't you skate home?' Then I added, 'Sorry, you see I thought that was a skateboard, but it's actually not.' I think he was Greek, in any case he definitely couldn't understand what I meant. It was all Greek to him. Or, you know, not Greek. Anyway, our disastrous back-and-forth left us both confused and a woman sharing the pole beside me sighed heavily into her Kindle. In the end I just rapped twice on the board and gestured to the boy to put his headphones back in.

Hestor made a new bank card and handed it to me. The card joined the gym card in my ever-improving wallet. I marvelled at the ease of it all. On my way out, I heard an old lady in a huge hat complaining loudly at the coffee stand, 'You still got no diabetic sugar here and a lot of us folks, you know, we need it.' I mimed a one-two combo at the security guard and he laughed and waved me goodbye.

This morning is really turning around, I thought. *I'm glad I didn't kill myself.*

Pink and Breathless

When it comes to nights out, no matter how delightful the invitation or fascinating the prospect is, the scenario that speaks loudest to me is always the one where I get to *stay in*. A little tug consistently pulls my heart and brain inside, back to solitude, back to comfort, back to back-to-back videos of Action Bronson. For work and for fun I understand that I must leave the house and yet I hear a faint song in the air, a ghostly voice, the spirit of a frail old black lady calling to me from the sofa, urging me to stay. 'Oh won't you stay with me?' she implores. 'I don't want you to leave, will you hold my hand?' She mentions a one-night stand and I'm taken aback, until I realise it's not a phantom at all – it's just the radio playing that poor creature Sam Smith begging a stranger for sex. No shame in that, my brother, but I must go out. That's right, I'm going out. I have to. In order to force myself out of the house against my very own will and instinct, I remind myself of certain things. Certain terrible things that happen only when you stay in.

One summer day when I was young … I'm still young now, of course, but this scenario happened when I was even younger than I am now, if you can even imagine that! Anyway, my girls (meaning my school friends including some boys and a dog) called to the house and asked me if I wanted to go and sit on the water tank behind the school with them. That was our version of 'going out'. I said no. I said I would not go out. I would stay in and help my mother. By 'help my mother' I meant I would pretend to clean the counter tops while waiting for my mother to discard bits of dough from the apple tarts she was making. I was obese as a pre-teen, so it just made sense.

Predictably, my mother trimmed the crust too close to the fruit. I wasn't about to complain, her mistake played right into my hands – the very hands that would soon be filled with raw pastry for me to dip in sugar and gobble up. Suddenly it all kicked off. There was a knock on the door and my mother asked me to run upstairs and get her cheque book so she could pay the milkman. That's not a euphemism. Anyway I ran upstairs and because of my aforementioned obesity, I quickly became pink and breathless. On my way back down I decided to jump the last three steps at once, to save time and energy. I did not realise that our new puppy was sleeping on the bottom step … only the sensation of her organs being crushed beneath my chubby feet alerted me.

Relax hippies, Rippy survived. But she was never the same confident little Madame she had been before the incident. She became afraid of apple tarts, the milkman and me and remained that way for the rest of her life. Jumping on a puppy is just one of the bad things that can happen when you stay in. I'm ashamed of myself still. Animal cruelty is no laughing matter, not even if you strap a turtle onto each foot and say, 'Look how slow my rollerblades are.'

I have an even more appalling example of what happens when you stay in. In the late 1990s, around the same time as I was stomping on young dogs' livers, Harrison Ford was working as a doctor with a beard when himself and his wife were invited to an event. He went out and had a great time. Oh there were canapés and drinks and clever little conversations. Harrison Ford's wife did not go out. What did she do instead? *She stayed in.* The poor thing seems to have been planning a romantic night in; that's an assumption based on the fact that there were rose petals sprinkled in the hallway and on the stairs leading to the bedroom (honk honk). Or perhaps the petals simply came from old flowers, maybe she was frugal and attempting to stretch the life of the flowers out by changing the water, getting her money's worth. Maybe after doing this, she was bringing the vase back upstairs and some of the petals brushed off the banister and fell onto the ground. The point is we will never know if she was being thrifty or being sexy because the glamorous brunette didn't live to clarify. A guy with a really cool haircut and just one real arm killed her, stone dead.

Now, was it such a great idea for her to stay in? While you consider your answer, here is some sarcasm:

I bet poor Mrs Dr Ford was thinking, *What fun, oh how hilarious, I'm getting killed by this one-armed man who used to go fishing with my husband's colleague. Oh, I'm so glad I didn't go to that party and eat the mini quiches and finish off the stories my hot husband set up for me and make everybody jealous of our cool telepathic connection and shared history of fun times, no way – this slow strangulation by a one-armed man is infinitely preferable.*

Everything is better outside your house. Take conversations, for example. Here is a classic conversation between my old roommate and me that happened inside the house.

ME

Can this go in recycling?

CONOR

I'm not sure. Maybe don't risk it.

Contrast that with a conversation between myself and a taxi driver that occurred that same night.

TAXI DRIVER

Where do you go, miss?

ME

Take me to Coney Island, sir.

That's right – only a bloody fun fair! The faded grandeur, the wooden pier, the salty air, the sweet nostalgia you feel despite having never been there before … are you seriously telling me it's better to stay in and miss a life made of cotton candy and bittersweet memories? No, no I won't believe it. I must go out. I can go out. I shall go out!

If You See Something, Say Something

I am furious. I am incandescent with rage. It's 2am and I absolutely cannot go to bed because of this burning anger and the accompanying sense of hopelessness that pervades my very being.

Twenty minutes ago, I didn't feel like this. I was happy back then. You should have seen me. Oh, let me tell you about that carefree girl before even the memory of her is obliterated by this new hell.

Twenty minutes ago, I was just in the door from a party, a party that was actually good because it contained the following human ingredients:

1. Three people you *don't* like so you have something to focus on.

2. Two people you *do* like so you can talk to them about the ones you don't and finally.
3. One person you *really* like.

Note: In case the italics I just deployed failed their mission, let me be clear about that last one – someone you want to put your Russian hands and Roman fingers all over, get it?

Tonight's party contained all the above ingredients, as well as an extra special one – me – bringing the yeast! Not literally, you understand, but I did help the party rise. I provided just the right amount of fizz and confidence to help create that mysterious alchemy that makes a party fun.

You must not forget that even the the best parties conceal many traps – tiny social deaths creep around every corner, stifling giggles as they wait for you to run into them. Anxieties multiply. Amongst strangers, simple things take on a new menace. The shared food: was it my turn to dip? I don't know. The conversational sinkholes: is there a difference between Hasidic and Orthodox Jews? Again, I don't know. Why did I ask? Was it because of his ringlets? Oh dear. Will they notice if I disappear for 40 minutes and go through their bathroom cabinet? What am I even looking for? Is Nurofen Plus an upper or a downer? Which of those do I even need?

Despite these horrors, I still go to parties from time to time because I don't know how else to find and collect great people, apart from tracking down YouTube commenters I feel a kinship with. When I move to a new place, it's hard not to feel like a little billygoat butting up against people, trying to convince them I'm worth knowing.

Earlier today my human instinct was, as it so often is, to skip the party and stay at home instead – possibly curled around a wheel of cheese lowing quietly to myself. That changed when I heard through the grapevine (my phone's nickname is 'The Grapevine') that a particular honey-pot I was hoping to get my paws around was going to this party. That's when my animal instinct took over. If you must know, my animal instinct is a mysterious but sexy cross between an owl and a silverback gorilla, and it must be obeyed. Its clear instruction tonight was to have a banana and read a book, as well as the new and urgent directive to *go to the honey pot before winter*. Who am I to disagree with those big eyes and strong shoulders? I put down the Comte and got dressed.

To say I didn't look great would be self-deprecating and we don't do that in America. Plus, worse than that, it would be a brazen lie. I want to be honest with you guys, OK? Is this a safe space? I hope so – because I want to tell you that I looked great. I wore all black and all tight, with a red lip. Actually, make it two red lips. The look I was going for was 'a jilted architect who is ready to love again … but you must be tender with her', crossed with 'sporty, maybe gay'. Overall – intriguing.

And I can say with confidence that almost everything went according to plan. First, I found the house on my own, although it was in an unfamiliar part of town. When I got there, I had a warm exchange with the birthday girl. Luckily she opened the door, so I didn't have to traipse through the crowd with a big dumb grin on my face while desperately scanning the room. I was careful not to monopolise her time and keep her away from the other guests.

I brought the ideal gift – a book I knew she would enjoy. 'You can read this on the train,' I told her – I didn't say, 'on the N to work,' so I came off as thoughtful, but not in a 'see, I listen to everything you say and note it down like a sociopath,' way.

I had a drink but didn't get drunk. I flirted (old-school, lots of hair twirling and sassy put-downs) with a nice guy with some sort of simple job on Wall Street. I made sure to do that well within earshot of the actual target – the Honey Pot. I met new people and was charming but also careful not to dominate the conversation. I didn't mention race in America. One girl I talked to absolutely had the potential to be a new friend – she seemed funny and interesting. Her job was making comedy theatre for sick kids. Not as useful as making them medicine, of course, but it cheers them up.

I made a real effort to be an effortless party girl and it worked out great, for me and the other party goers. I left at exactly the right time and didn't make a fuss about it. Neither did I slip out quietly – I said my goodbyes discreetly, like a good guest.

Last, but not least, I resisted the cake. I have shocked you with that last declaration, I'm sure. Maybe you're thinking, *Well, we don't know how good the cake was so we can't know how difficult it was for you to resist it.* Hear me now: if you're like me and parties make you anxious, and you're prone to over-eating when anxious, then you go to a party and there's cake at that party, it doesn't matter how good the cake is, you'll eat it. Yet I didn't.

I can hear you bleating, 'How, but but – how did you manage to ignore it?' Relax, babe. I'll tell you. I had taken precautions, you see. I had brought some almonds in my handbag, and as I was locking up my bike to go in, I ate a giant handful of them. That was at about 9pm.

A good dose of almonds makes you feel pretty full for absolutely ages, they are magic like that. My ultimate favourite nut is the macadamia, because it's creamy and sweet and oily all at the same time. They are my treat nuts. Almonds are my go-to, work-horse nuts for filling in the gaps between meal times and, crucially, preventing confectionery panic eats. My 14-year-old self would have shot me in the head for being so tedious as to categorise nuts in this way. I don't care, she was wrong about Oasis and she was wrong about not caring about anything. The 32-year-old me was proud of remembering to have almonds and confident that they would see me through my triumphant evening of socialising.

But at what cost?

The thing is, the almonds were unblanched and in their skins.

I do have a winning smile, but, to be honest, my teeth are quite tightly packed together and I often get food stuck in them. I didn't wear my retainer, OK? Is that OK with you?

I am usually rigorous in my approach to checking them. I carry a little mirror with me like a 1940s starlet (actress, not car), but this evening I was so distracted by locking my bike up against thieves, I didn't think to look for debris.

When I got home from the party a little while ago, after I'd sat on my front step and relived the glory of it all for a few minutes, I came inside to wash my face and congratulate myself some more. I smiled at my reflection in the mirror – I mean, why not, right? I'll tell you why not. That smile revealed to me something I cannot now un-see. A large fleck of goddamned brown almond skin tucked neatly between my incisor and canine teeth.

I had eaten the almonds four hours previously. Oh, the anguish as the sharp pain of realisation dulls into a lasting ache of foolishness.

The trained detectives among you will have already done the maths and reached the same dreadful conclusion as myself – the almond skin had been lodged there, making a fool out of me, for the entire duration of the party.

So now you understand why I sit here angrily, railing against the dark night and reeling from the irrefutable fact that nobody told me I had something in my teeth.

I can't help running through the whole evening in my mind, over and over. I'm especially mad at the first person I spoke to at the party, the birthday girl.

I wouldn't be sitting here now with hot tears of fury in my eyes if she had simply spared a moment to tap her own teeth and look at me with raised eyebrows. That was all it would have taken!

I can see it now. I would have whipped out my compact, turned away and flicked off the offending brown impostor, and got back to business.

But, no, oh no. Too easy! That would have involved her looking past her own predicament for a second, and she was so taken up with her party, her birthday, her life quickly marching towards the inevitable, that she could not possibly spare that moment, that tiny moment. A tap? A look? Oh no – far too much to ask for.

Again, I hear the laughter of those little knots of people as I wisecracked my way around the room – only this time I wonder what they were really laughing at.

I'm not forgetting my so-called new best friend, the blasted children's entertainer. Couldn't she have dropped the Patch Adams act for a second and helped a sister out? That would have been real charity.

I'm doubled over with agony now, as I remember my shameless flirting with that idiotic trader, all the while unaware of the humiliation of the unmentionable almond skin. That 'nice guy' I was telling you about – the one I was using to attract someone else's attention? Not so nice after all, was he now? Bloody Judas!

And crucially, what of my love interest, the Honey Pot? Did my wild eyes and poor dental hygiene throw him? Is that why he wouldn't take off his top? I despair. I hope I never see any of those people again. I'm going to bed. Right after I brush my teeth so hard I spit blood.

An Alien of
Extraordinary Ability

The O-1 nonimmigrant visa is for the individual who possesses extraordinary ability in the sciences, arts, education, business, or athletics, or who has a demonstrated record of extraordinary achievement in the motion picture or television industry and has been recognised nationally or internationally for those achievements.
United States Citizenship and Immigration Services

Of all the visas in all the world, this is the visa I had the best chance of getting. Let me not bother you with false modesty and protestations of 'Who me? Little old me? Sure there is nothing extraordinary about me at all at all, I'm as normal as they come,' etc. I will show no such coyness, because I have got extraordinary abilities and I am not going to hide my light under any bushel by neglecting to mention them. Here they are, in no particular order.

1. I can think of puns very quickly and with little effort. Let's say we're talking about pop stars as service providers. OK, I am putting 30 seconds on the clock. Here we go.
   — Tailor Swift (repairs clothes in a hurry)
   — Katie Periwinkle-Picker (picks periwinkles)
   — Usher (ushers)

2. I can tell when someone wants someone else's job on a TV production.

3. I can skim through a book and still make a convincing argument that it was 'not that great' that same night at book club.

4. I know upon seconds of seeing the first plates of dim sum arriving to the table whether or not more need dim sum need to be ordered.

5. I can sense when a comedian needs to stop doing comedy.

6. I know the exact right time to order more dim sum so that we are just finishing the first plates when the next round arrives.

Much to my disgust, none of these skills was deemed worthy of President Obama's special attention, and I had to go through the regular channels, and provide actual evidence of all these other extraordinary abilities.

EVIDENTIARY CRITERIA FOR O-1B VISA

Evidence that the beneficiary has received, or been nominated for, significant national or international awards or prizes in the particular field, such as an Academy Award, Emmy, Grammy or Director's Guild Award.

Sit down, I'm warning you, if you don't you may keel over. Look, I've never received or even been nominated for *any* of the above awards. It's strange to me too. After all my work on a hidden camera show, all of those moving scenes where I wore a fake baby bump and chased men down the street to get one of their hairs as a DNA sample – that only got me an IFTA. An IFTA is an Irish Film and Television Award. Does that count? It's sort of like an Oscar except very different. No Nobel Prize for Literature for me, even after all the jokes about my cat Little Edie and that fine essay in my first book about my gluten sensitivity. A lot of great artists don't get their rewards until they're dead. Well, consider me dead. I don't mean that, but I am hoping to pick up at least a Grammy for my new role as a giant self-loathing doll for the wonderful animated series *Doc McStuffins.*

OR evidence of at least three of the following:

- *Performed and will perform services as a lead or starring participant in productions or events which have a distinguished reputation as evidenced by critical reviews, advertisements, publicity releases, publications, contracts or endorsements.*

I was booked in for a few shows in a Brooklyn bar, a place called Union Hall that I adore – with bocce ball lanes on the ground floor and a small performance space in the basement. I would be the starring participant, and as we had yet to sell any tickets, perhaps I would be the only or 'lead' participant too! The production – a comedy show – had yet to build a distinguished reputation because it hadn't actually started. The tricky thing about this criterion is that you must organise and plan lots of fancy productions and events to prove how needed you are, but you have to do so before you even apply for a visa. It's a real chicken and egg scenario, your career being the chicken, your legal status the egg.

- *Achieved national or international recognition for achievements, as shown by critical reviews or other published materials by or about the beneficiary in major newspapers, trade journals, magazines, or other publications.*

I collected the recommended 40 pages of press. It was tortuous. Before you slam this book down and spray me with a big red 'P' for privileged, let me say that I understand how difficult other immigrants have it coming into the US, I do. I know that reading a lukewarm review of my 2007 Edinburgh Fringe show does not compare with paying a coyote all of the money your family has ever earned just for a chance at crossing the deadly Mexican border. What I had to do was nothing compared to a Syrian refugee applying for asylum having been displaced by war and left with nowhere to go.

The grotesque thing is that I, as a white Westerner, always had a better chance than those people, who clearly need it more, of starting a new life in the good old US of A.

That said, reading other people's opinions of my work is unpleasant. Not that I believe everything that's written – I don't, particularly not the good stuff. And as for the bad, my inner critic has access to what's really going on and relishes saying things that are much more incisive and damaging than anything an external critic could dream up. In fact, it's a pure balm to get their surface-level reproaches. The reason I don't like reading press about my comedy is that it makes me self-conscious. It makes me think about what I'm up to and how I'm being perceived by others. I worry that when I'm thinking about it, it changes. I'm not sure I have the bulldozer gene, the one that says 'strike ahead no matter what they say'.

It's important to me to be as close to myself onstage as possible. Of course it will never be total reality. When

I step on to a stage and amplify my voice and command everyone to listen to me and only me – that's not exactly me up there, it's a version of me, a persona. I still try to make it as unselfconscious as possible and the more layers of inhibition there are, the more difficult that becomes. Having read all the press I could find and selected the most positive and flattering to show to the US government, my stand-up suffered for a few months. After researching the public's opinion of me for two weeks, it began to show on stage, where I am often most comfortable. I couldn't help it, an adjective that I'd read about myself would pop into my head and I would feel furious as I tried to be less or more of that adjective.

- *A record of major commercial or critically acclaimed successes, as shown by such indicators as title, rating or standing in the field, box office receipts, motion picture or television ratings and other occupational achievements reported in trade journals, major newspapers or other publications.*

  I made a TV show called *Fancy Vittles* with my sister Lilly; we made one series and it didn't get picked up because it was too niche. I did have good reviews though, so I flinchingly scanned them. So, a commercial success, no, critical one, yes – this is an odd feeling. It's like getting an extreme haircut and everyone swooning over it and telling you how great you look, but then nobody gets the same haircut. They just stay the way they've always been, with a flattering layered bob.

- *Received significant recognition for achievements from organisations, critics, government agencies or other recognised experts in the field in which the beneficiary is engaged, with the testimonials clearly indicating the author's authority, expertise and knowledge of the beneficiary's achievements.*

  These are known as 'The Twelve Letters'. This is a mortifying process for anyone remotely insecure about their worth as a person and an artist. For example, a woman, or an Irish person, or a person who was raised Catholic. Let me explain what these letters are. I cannot relive it because it is too embarrassing, so I will give you the information in the form of advice:

— You must ask people to vouch for you, in writing, to the Department of Homeland Security. Not just anybody, they must be supremely successful and way above you on the scale of one to show business.

— Your lawyer will give you sample letters to pass on to the people you are asking for help from, and you will crawl under the stairs and lie there quietly after you've read them.

— These letters are brimful of hyperbole. They have to be, to convince the officer in charge of your case that you are indeed an alien of extraordinary ability.

Words like 'magnificent', 'peerless' and 'transcendent' are encouraged.

— Consider taking regular doses of cocaine throughout this letter-collecting phase, or at least start injecting testosterone.

- *A high salary or other substantial remuneration for services in relation to others in the field, as shown by contracts or other reliable evidence.*

In the past I definitely had a high salary, for months at a time! That's back when I was ballin' but not anymore, now I'm just bawlin' … bawlin' cryin'. At the time I applied for this visa, I had agents and managers in three different countries *and* a babysitting job.

So as you've probably figured out, I was extremely lucky. Thanks to my good fortune and lots of help from my friends, I got this visa. Now I'm here and running for Mayor of New York City under a strong anti-immigration ticket. The last thing I need is a flood of white comedians trying to make it in the Big Apple.

Not My Place to Say

I do stand-up comedy because being funny is important to me and also because comedy helps me figure out how I feel about things, it can be a way to process my day. As you can imagine, this can go either way. I did a spot at a show in Williamsburg, Brooklyn the same December day that a grand jury decided not to indict the white police officer who put an unarmed black man, Eric Garner, in a choke hold on a Staten Island street that July, a choke hold that killed him. There were protests kicking off across the city, people were staging die-ins in Grand Central Station and taking over the West Side Highway.

The comics on before me had addressed the day's events in an oblique way. One white comic mentioned 'anti-police feelings' and shared a story of the time he was fined because he'd crossed the street while the light was red. I was up after him, and got on stage feeling the way I'd felt all day, namely angry and confused, very confused. I had moved to New York a year previously, and always tried to avoid the lazy comedy that relies on 'the differences between Ireland and America'. I also felt conflicted about criticising a country that had welcomed me so generously, but that night, I did both of those things.

In Ireland the police force are called An Garda Síochána, meaning 'The Guardians of the Peace'. They are not perfect, but they're also not armed. Most members of the Garda Síochána are equipped with batons and pepper spray but only detective units carry guns. I used to do jokes about this back home, imagining a poor chubby Garda running after a criminal but soon giving up the chase, perhaps calling out after the criminal, 'Oh, please come back– sir? Could you just … Oh, never mind.' I thought it was sort of quaint and nice. I didn't realise it was important.

I began my set by saying that in Ireland the police do not kill the people they are supposed to protect and serve. I said that in America the police sometimes *do* kill the people they are supposed to protect and serve. And those people are usually black. I said that I wasn't sure that the guns are the only problem. It was true that just that August, Michael Brown, an unarmed black teenager, was shot six times by Officer Darren Wilson, but Eric Garner was killed with Officer Daniel Pantaleo's bare hands.

I talked haltingly and not very funnily about how my

experience with the NYPD was limited to smiling exchanges. I talked about how, because I am a white woman, I am not afraid that the police will harass or even kill me but that if I were black, I would be.

All of this, at a comedy show? Damn. I burnt it to the ground. I genuinely felt sorry for the audience, having to listen to me figuring out my feelings on race and privilege and the NYPD. But also – I needed to talk about it. It seemed too weird *not* to talk about it. The vibe I got from the young, almost all white crowd of hipsters was vague uneasiness, a sort of embarrassment, like, 'Yeah – we've all retweeted Ta-Nehisi Coates on this and we all feel terrible … but it's sort of not cool to bring it up right now.'

To end my set I tried to lift spirits with a routine I was working on about how if I was rich I would own an ostrich and have it wait for me outside cafes, but my heart wasn't in it. The unenviable job of following me fell to a comic out of DC who thankfully managed to break the tension I'd created. He addressed my set, thanked me for talking about it and said it sounded like I had some understanding 'maybe because the Irish are the niggas of Europe'. The audience seemed relieved that a black man said it was OK for me to talk about what was happening outside.

I appreciated my fellow comic's words, but I didn't agree with him because the thing is, I *don't* understand. Long ago, yes, the Irish were colonised by England and brutalised by her law enforcers. People living in the North of Ireland fared worse, for longer, and the repercussions are still being felt there.

Today though, here in America, Irish people are just fine; more than that, we are firmly part of the establishment and very safe in our whiteness. My experience of this city is wholly different to that of my black neighbour. Eric Garner being brutally killed and the injustice of his killer not *even* being tried in court had suddenly brought into focus just how different my experience of living in America is to a black person's.

The gig limped on, the next comic bantering with a drunken heckler who told him she sold soup for a living, before she fell asleep on her date's shoulder. After him, the closer did a solid routine about a man farting on an airplane. Everybody filed out, headed for the L train, buttoning up down-filled coats as they walked past bakeries selling gluten-free cupcakes and apartment buildings where a one-bedroom will set you back $4000 a month.

I got the train too, feeling more mixed up than ever. I felt I had made a cultural misstep in speaking about something I was not entitled to discuss. I don't doubt that the other white people in the room were just as horrified by the day's news as I was, but they either didn't want to talk about it or didn't know how. Their reaction put me in mind of the way people sometimes react to a grieving family after a tragic loss. They ignore them, unable to handle the reality of it, unwilling to join in the pain, all the while insisting they are just allowing them space.

Alice Walker wrote, 'The most common way people give up their power is by thinking they don't have any.' What she did not write about is how much easier it is to stay in that ignorant space; deciding that it's not your place to say is the perfect excuse to remain silent.

When it comes to systematic racism, 'what if it were me?' is a question white people in America never have to consider. I thought about that; in the almost impossible to imagine scenario of me being choked to death on the street by an NYPD officer, I would want everyone to care. I would want the world to stop spinning and only start again when the truth had been told, some kind of justice done. How devastating if the only people who made any noise about my death were other white people. How terrible if everyone else turned away, muttering that they felt bad about it, but what could they do?

Making Scents of It All

Whenever I see a stylish woman I admire, I look for ways to emulate her so I can be fabulous too. I ask her questions, trying to capture just where her charm lies, and how I can get it for myself. Some of my recent queries to these Queens include:

— Where did you get your skirt?
— How did you find your smile?
— Do you actually feel beguiling, if so what is that like?
— What is the brand and shade of nail polish on your nails, please?

This last question is easy, one they can often answer. I take their words and dash off to get my nails done in Essie's 'Blushing Bride', which is one shade away from 'Sugar Daddy'. Other Essie shades include the commanding 'Tuck

It in My Tux', the artless, 'Show Me the Ring' and the hopeful, 'Meet Me at the Altar', alongside the thrilling, 'Brides to Be'. The man really is the cure in every manicure. It's almost as if women are still expected to aspire to marriage! I try on the skirt, my nails are right, I practice my smile in the mirror. Despite all of this, I still can't put my finger on just what they've got. It's a certain … I don't know what. The French probably have a word for this mysterious element that so few possess, or perhaps they don't know what to call it either.

Perhaps it is scent. Invisible to the eye but all-powerful, how a person smells can often be why I am drawn to them. When it comes to smells, I am quite traditional. I like my men to smell of fresh air and education. I like my old ladies to smell of mints and starch and I like my babies to smell of Christina Aguilera's 'Red Sin'. Well, either 'Red Sin' or else just smell like babies. Famously, babies smell terrific. Somehow, getting sick on themselves and sleeping all day works out great for them. Classic double standard there; when I get sick on myself and sleep all day people get all sanctimonious and say things like, 'Just get your feet on the floor, babe, hop in the shower and start your day.'

Babies really do get away with murder. If you're a true crime fan or a detective reading this, maybe you're wondering just how a baby, with their lack of co-ordination, would commit a murder. Well, they could distract you by speaking an unexpected language, that always throws me. When this tiny person speaks French, it is so surprising one could easily take a step back from the pram, then wham! You get hit by a milk truck. Babies could pretend to be taking tummy time and use the opportunity to steady a rifle with their little torsos and blammo! Believe me, they have their ways, and those big eyes just serve to hide their guilt.

Babies might smell divine but they make me nervous, I tend to witter on in front of them. You know when you're thrown together with someone at a party and there is a discreet agreement between you both to carry the conversational load? Babies don't bother. They are happy to be spoken *about*, particularly in glowing terms, but rarely do they actually contribute *to* the conversation. They care little for etiquette and just stare, while I fill the silence. Once, after a particularly chilling showdown with a one-year-old in a café, I had to break the impasse and I did so with a lie. Like many lies, this one was not premeditated; I was surprised to hear it myself. After three tense minutes of me reading my book and squirming under his constant gaze, the baby's mother said, 'Hugo likes you!' I got up, smiled and said, 'Well, Hugo – I've got to go home and walk my little doggie.' I don't have a dog. I don't even have a plant. Now I'm worried that I will see him again, and his mother will say, 'There's the nice lady with the doggie.' Then I'll be forced to make something up and say something like, 'Oh that doggie was eaten by a badger, end of story.'

Enough about babies! See how they dominate without even being present? Tiny cute demons! Now, back to the subject in question: babies. No. No, I beg your pardon. I meant to say smells. In Al Pacino's wonderful biopic *Scent of a Woman*, I learned that the celebrated actor is also a retired army colonel. He is visually impaired so his nose steps in and sees things for him. In a particularly riveting scene, he breaks women down into our various physical parts and explains to his carer, a young Chris O'Donnell lookalike, how nice we smell. It seems like maybe he's objectifying us and that doesn't feel great, but sometimes you just have to say to yourself, 'Give the guy a break, he's just an old, blind actor who (spoiler alert) wants to kill himself.'

I want my own scent, and have been experimenting with an assortment of them. In fact, I bought perfume last year and wore it for weeks before realising it was my mother's signature scent. Initially, I panicked about what that meant for me, psychologically, but then I turned it around and used it to my advantage. I sat with my siblings in darkened rooms and they opened up to me like never before. In the same way a farmer tricks a lamb by covering a ewe with another ewe's musky pelt, they thought I was their beloved mamma. Then I switched on the lamps and laughed long and hard at their little concerns and big plans.

When my mother would go to dinner dances around Christmas time, she would get all dressed up and put on lipstick and a necklace, then she would spray perfume in front of her and walk through it. That enchanted mist would set the tone. My father never wore cologne. On special occasions he would put Brylcreem in his hair, but that was the extent of his primping. Still, he always smelled great – clean and safe. The only time that changed was after one summer afternoon, when he put petrol on a bonfire to hurry it up a bit. The flames leapt up and singed his eyebrows off and he smelled quite smoky for a few days after that, but soon reclaimed his dependable freshness.

I want to smell special and unmistakably *me* to the point that people will sniff the air and say, '*She* has been here, you know – whatshername.' However, the qualities I like the most about myself don't necessarily lend themselves to a smell. Funny is my favourite way to be, but do I want to smell funny? I don't know that I want people to say, 'Let's buy a ticket to see Maeve, that girl even smells funny!'

I want to smell sensual and elegant, like a woman who rarely falls over. I think and think about my favourite smells. I like the smell of roast chicken and lemon and thyme and caramelised onions. Basically: gravy, your basic gravy.

I want to have a unique aroma that can send me places, because I believe that smell is the sense that allows us to travel through time. I wonder if I want to smell like the past;

my childhood best friend's auburn hair close to my face on a sleepover, my granddad's coffee and oranges, Ballybrassil Strand. Or should I aim for the scent of the future? All I can do is guess what that would be. Prison perhaps, or a divine hug from Oprah?

My dream fragrance will not disguise me – it will reveal my essence, my core, it will uncover something more private even than my browsing history. (*Codeine. Jake Gyllenhaal no T-shirt. What is codeine in? Get codeine night time. Jake Gyllenhaal no jumper*). Once I find it, I will spray that hope-filled bouquet before me in an ivory bedroom, then sail right through it like a mighty ship, out the front door – stopping only to dab a little on my cold sore, for luck.

I was walking down Broome Street with my friend Abi when she said excitedly, 'Come over here, this is the smelliest block in Manhattan!' I didn't notice anything out of the ordinary. It was a real stinker of a block, but the rest of the street smelled bad too, and it was only May. The heat of the summer ripens the trash and stirs up the ammoniac smell of cat piss, rotten vegetables and petrol.

My friend George, a long time New Yorker, despises people who come to the city and complain that it's too cold in the winter and it stinks in the summer. 'Fuck them, man. It's New York City what do they think is gonna happen?' I nod sagely. Perhaps I even add a, 'Yeah, fuck *them*,' for good measure. What did I think was going to happen? There is nowhere to put the trash except out on the street, and it's baking hot. So it follows that the place will sometimes reek. George typifies the attitude a lot of New Yorkers have. A stoicism that says if you want to live here, you just have to deal with it. Smells, noise, rushing, there is competition even for air. I wonder if I can deal with it, and for how long.

In a city this packed with buildings and technology, the natural world gets pushed around. The day after the stinkiest block tour, I have a meeting at a media company on Flatbush Avenue. A truck chugs past and there's something wrong with the exhaust, the fumes fill my nose as I ring the office bell. While I wait to be buzzed in, I hear a chirruping sound coming from the sill above my head. I am excited to think they have a nest of sparrows under their eaves, but when I ask about the sound a producer tells me it is a recording, placed there by an artist to remind New Yorkers of the birds who once lived there. This unexpected infusion of melancholy travels through my heart and into my day. It makes me annoyed, as feelings tend to do. *I thought it was a real bird!* I grumble to myself. *A cool Brooklyn bird coming up in Biggie's old neighbourhood, catching a Nets game, eating scraps of cheesecake from Junior's.*

After the meeting I go to Central Park, way uptown, the 96th Street entrance. It's after 6pm and the sting of heat has gone. I clamber up some gently sloping rocks, then lie in the cleft of the biggest one. It is solid and warm under my skin as I look up at a sassafras tree. Some bugs are buzzing above my head but I don't look to see what they are. A Red Admiral lands near me and I put out my hand to see if it will investigate, but it deftly flits away. There is a sweet little trilling coming from the branches and I wonder what kind of bird is making it. Or is it an artist's speaker? All thoughts drift away as my mind stills. Down from the rocks and across the way a family packs up after a picnic, the little ones scampering after every blown-along napkin. A group of teenagers walk by, boys with basketballs, jostling and shouting. Planes are tiny, busy in the sky, drivers honk their horns close by on Fifth and far off sirens do their rounds. The air smells sweet. This city is nature too, full of living, breathing beings that make up a world that's humming now as it lulls me to sleep.

Acknowledgements

Thank you to my family, especially the babies. Thank you to my book club, especially the ladies. Thank you to the following people who did various amazing things to help me write this book. Ciara Considine, Kevin Townley, Mara Altman, Olivia Wingate, Faith O'Grady, Avra and Dahlia Greenspan, Kristen Schaal, Chigozie Obioma, Shaina Feinberg, Carolyn Altman, Róisín Ingle, Phoebe Robinson, Claudia O'Doherty, Jon Ronson, Brian Rogers, Chenoa Estrada, Cath Gagon, Julie Meyer, Marianne Ways, Julie Smith, Ramit Kreitner, Maggie Armstrong and Avra and Dahlia Greenspan, Emma Dunne, Patrick Freyne.